DATE DUE

D0894047

Randall Jarrell on W. H. Auden

Randall Jarrell
on W.H. Auden

Edited by

Stephen Burt

with **Hannah Brooks-Motl**

 Columbia University Press   New York

Columbia University Press
Publishers Since 1893
New York   Chichester, West Sussex

Copyright © 2005 Columbia University Press
All rights reserved
Copyright page continued after the index, page 179.

Library of Congress Cataloging-in-Publication Data
Jarrell, Randall, 1914–1965
    Randall Jarrell on W. H. Auden / edited by Stephen Burt with
Hannah Brooks-Motl.
      p.   cm.
    Includes bibliographical references and index.
    ISBN 0–231–13078–3 (acid-free paper)
    1. Auden. W. H. (Wystan Hugh), 1907–1973 — Criticism and interpretation.
I. Burt, Stephen, 1971– II. Brooks-Motl, Hannah. III. Title.
PR6001.U4Z7534 2005
811'.52 — dc22

2004061787

Columbia University Press books are printed on permanent
   and durable acid-free paper.

Printed in the United States of America
c 10 9 8 7 6 5 4 3 2 1

Contents

Foreword

Two Poets

Adam Gopnik

To read Randall Jarrell on W. H. Auden is to read the best-equipped of American critics of poetry of the past century on the best-equipped of its Anglo-American poets, and we rush to read, perhaps, less out of an academic interest in fair judgment than out of a spectator's love of virtuosity in flight. In flight rather than in fight—for all that these rescued lectures are in principle an "attack" by one poet on another, the effect is less of a battle joined than of two virtuosi playing side by side: like Menuhin and Grapelli playing jazz standards. It is a cutting contest without cuts, an occasion of witticisms more than a battle of wits. Most readers will no longer have much doubt but that Jarrell was "wrong" on one level—Auden's poems of the mid-1940s, his later manner, continue to inspire critics and delight readers—and so we fall on these lectures not for their strictures and shapes but for their lines, in the hope that Jarrell will be Jarrell throughout as much as Auden will go on being Auden afterward.

And Jarrell does not disappoint; he is in dreamy peak form from beginning to end. Though some of the lines are familiar to us from the long pieces that were extracted from these lectures, most are not. The intent, almost comically detailed analysis of the transformation of Auden's rhetoric in the 1940s remains as good as any we have— as good an instance of a critic reading a poet as we have—and better still is the tone. " I really felt so gay-serious, competent and inspired while I talked, " Jarrell wrote to his wife Mary in the midst of the lectures, and gay-serious is exactly what the lectures are. What can we do save melt when we read, for instance, from lecture 6, anent *Paid on Both Sides*: "Anybody *can* make discursive statements about poems—half the people I know start making discursive statements a block and a half before they reach the poems. But to read the poems, really to read them—that *is* difficult. We are judging the poems, all right, but the poems are also judging us—and I hope my hearers will give *Paid on Both Sides* plenty of time to judge them, and not give it a chance to say, 'Yeah, the usual sort of readers . . . Next!' "

It is, surely, this atmosphere of high-spirited play throughout that disarms even the Auden-loving reader. Auden himself, though he can't exactly have liked the treatment, seems to have accepted it in this spirit. At least, there is no record of the kind of vendetta that such occasions usually call up, or even of the normal requisite two weeks' annoyance. Phillip Larkin's "attack" on the same Auden poems is fairly called one, and though one laughs at Larkin's jokes, because they are good, and values his direct, terse hatred of fancy speech, still there is something distasteful in Larkin's words on Auden, reminding us of Larkin's limitations—the narrowness of sympathy so touching in Larkin's poems where his narrowness is dramatized as comedy, but that can, in his prose, touch the edge of the philistine. But with Jarrell on Auden one feels less in the presence of an unjust judgment than of a strange obsessive pleading, so that the result is in the end more like Kafka's letter to his father than like, say, any of the famous assaults of one poet on another, or like Jarrell's own assaults on Aiken or Cummings.

But these lectures are not simply a "performance"; the indictment Jarrell directs at Auden is urgent and heartfelt and touches on subjects that, independent of Auden, remain important to our idea of what poems are and do. Jarrell really does read the poems, and at the core of his reading is an argument about the rhetorical and romantic impulses in poetry, and how to get their balance right. Jarrell's argument, essentially, is that Auden had, in the long American poems of the 1940s, gone from being a cryptic, feeling, impassioned poet to a rhetorical, self-conscious one, from a poet who depends on experience to a poet who depends on devices, tricks. Jarrell's maniacally detailed inventory of every one of Auden's devices—including such things as "The Bureaucratization of Incongruity by Perspective"—bends toward a simple point: "All these lists of devices must by now have forced a generalization upon my hearers: that in his later poems Auden depends to an extraordinary degree upon rhetorical devices." He then asks, "How conscious and rational and controlled is poetry? can poetry afford to be? . . . there is in poetry something deep, obscure, and powerful that can neither be explained nor disregarded."

The indictment is, at one level, obviously true. Auden in the 1940s *was* a highly rhetorical poet who had worked out for himself a theory of why heartfelt poetry needed, in modern times, to be rhetorical, self-conscious, and ironic and "wrought." The long poems of the 1940s that Jarrell treats to such loving, alarmed dissection all involve ironic form and passionate feeling. The Christian vision in "For the Time Being" is filtered through pop-song parody and music-hall pastiche, while Swiftian couplets do the same estranging work in *New Year Letter*, and the drunk New Yorkers in the dive in *The Age of Anxiety* are made to speak Anglo-Saxonish alliterative verse. (It is telling that Bernstein's *Age of Anxiety* symphony, inspired by the Auden poem, feels as much of a period piece as Richard Rodgers's *Victory at Sea* does now, precisely because it is written throughout in a 1940s musical idiom; the odd, old style Auden chose is what keeps the poem young.) This is a practice that, in the intervening years, has become both more prevalent—so that the use of heavily advertised rhetorical devices has become almost a postmodern tic—and more vulnerable, helping to lead to the inevitable rise of the confessional or direct-speech schools that Jarrell's great friend and

sometime hero Lowell helped create (which have, one need hard-
ly add, rhetorical devices of their own). Jarrell, of course, under-
stood exactly what Auden was up to—that understanding and that
exactitude are the subject of these lectures and what make them so
much fun to read. But what is striking is the passion with which Jar-
rell insists that the practice is not just queer but *wrong*—that Auden
was a man with a wooden leg changing the rules of football to in-
sist that the game was all along meant only for men with wooden
legs, while healthy men with working feet watched from the side-
line and were made to think, "How dazzlingly perverse! I wish I
could lose my leg, too."

Fifty years on, a puzzling sense of what Jarrell missed comes to
the reader's mind as he turns these pages. Jarrell, such a witty writer,
has almost no feeling for either of the two traditions of wit in Eng-
lish writing. There is, after all, a tradition of the highest kind in
English of poems that are rhetorical, abstract, intellectual, hugely
self-conscious, and yet still funny, permanent, and effective; the "Es-
say on Man" or "The Vanity of Human Wishes" are obviously mod-
els for the 1940s Auden, and it would be nice to know why Jarrell
thinks that these poems work in a way that the *New Year Letter* does
not. Jarrell does say, quite explicitly, that *New Year Letter* "is no com-
petition for Pope," but his *reasons* for saying this lack his usual par-
ticularity. "It lacks the necessary immediacy and finality of presen-
tation, it is at a remove; the urgency and reality have been
diluted. . . . we feel that the poem, and everything else, is going to
be All Right In The End." Since these particular objections, includ-
ing the complaint about fatuous optimism, are exactly the ones that
readers have been directing at Pope since *his* worldly, rhetorical
verse first appeared, it is hard to see why Auden should be made to
suffer here by comparison.

Nor does Jarrell seem to like much, or see as a challenge to his
ideas about rhetoric and feeling in this context, the other famous
tradition of artificial poetry in English—for all that it was, unlike the
Augustan tradition, madly fashionable in the early 1950s—and that
of course is the tradition of the "Metaphysicals" of the seventeenth
century. Why Donne should be allowed his conceits and Auden be

disbarred from his is not something that Jarrell is inclined to argue
at length. This is strange, since what Auden did, in truth, is to put
the elaborate weird-metaphor making of the Metaphysicals into the
discursive public verse of the Augustans (the best bits of *New Year
Letter* read like George Herbert being channeled by Alexander Pope,
a weird, inward-turning Christian mystic speaking in genial public
garb). If we could have been in that lecture room in Princeton, it
might have been nice to ask, after the applause died down, *Okay, so
Auden's not the Thomas Hardy of the pylons, or even the Shelley of the documen-
tary films. He's rhetorical and full of conceits. He's like Donne, he's like Pope, he's
like Marvell. What's not to love about that?* That Auden did everything
that Jarrell describes is beyond argument; that he was wrong to do
this is, one feels, asserted more than argued.

And then, leaving the lecture room or sitting down for a drink
with the lecturer, our thoughts might turn to a deeper and less aca-
demic oddity; for the real irony that haloes these lectures is our dis-
concerting knowledge that Jarrell's gift, too, was for complicated
rhetoric—that we have here a master of rhetoric disparaging the
possible role of rhetoric in poetry, a wit crying out for less of it. Au-
den's problem, as Jarrell explicates it, was Jarrell's problem too. Jar-
rell was not a straight talker alarmed by a wise guy; he was one wise
guy alarmed by another. Jarrell was, even at this point in his evolu-
tion, still at times an almost pathologically rhetorical poet. And a
critic, of course, particularly an epigrammatic, aphoristic critic like
Jarrell, is of necessity rhetorical before anything else. Yet he was al-
ready and would remain drawn to the (seemingly) plainspoken, par-
ticular, and direct, to the naked, to Bishop and Frost and Lowell.
(Not that Bishop and Frost and Lowell are not all in their way
rhetorical poets, in the simple sense that each has a style and has
worked hard to have it. But we rarely say, reading Bishop, "How *does*
she do it," but simply, "How did she *know?*"

Jarrell was a poet as much as, and before, he was a critic, and his
own practice is, as it always is when poets speak on other poets, the
real subject of these lectures. For the reader who knows what Jarrell
will write later, reading these lectures is almost like watching a man
give a sympathetic, tender account of a friend writhing in a strait-

jacket while (chattily, engagingly, amusingly) he slips on one of his own and knots the sleeves in back. Jarrell asserts Auden's sins, one realizes, because he accepted as plain faith the primacy of romantic poetry—of a poetry of plain feeling and apprehended immediate experience—at a time when he was unable to write it. (How proudly he boasts that Hannah Arendt praised his poetry for its "nakedness and directness," not virtues much in show in these beautifully baroque lectures.) He is explicit about this without, perhaps, defending it—that he does not need to defend it is part of the strength of his belief. This belief not only creates a barrier between Auden and himself, it also creates a barrier between Jarrell's own poetry and his prose. That barrier, one comes to feel, is one of the hidden subjects in these lectures. Jarrell's prose, so full of ideas and opinions and judgment, is, at this stage of his work, almost completely absent from his still very wrought and at times obscure poetry.

So, though the ostensible argument here is about rhetoric, the real argument is about sincerity. Both Auden and Jarrell were stuck with the same problem: making peace with their wit without being merely witty. Auden solved it by a complicated poetry of expanded conceits addressing celestial matter, an ironic poetry of sincere devotions. Jarrell would, eventually and only toward the end of his life in the 1960s, solve the same problem. He would do it, in *The Lost World* particularly, by turning wit into comedy and letting comedy do the work that rhetoric had once done. He became a major poet only when he began to make his poems into comedies instead of poems, and they became poems. He was still naked and direct, but he was also dressed up and winning, and the tension between the emotion of his poetry and the suave intelligence taken over from his prose is what gives his last poems their authority.

In the end, Jarrell did make peace with his own wit—and one can't help but feel that Auden's example, so excoriated here, must have helped. For if there was one poet who was also dressed up at one moment and naked the next, who could show how a loss of conscious solemnity might point the way toward another kind of seriousness, it was Auden. One would not call poems like "A Man Meets a Woman on the Street" or "The Lost Children" witty as one

would call "Lakes" or " Under Which Lyre" witty. But Jarrell's later
poems become, to their great gain, funny and genial in ways that
the earlier Jarrell, the Jarrell of these lectures, did not yet know
how to be in verse. Auden's and Jarrell's were different solutions,
but both had the common effect of humanizing intellect, of taking
sensibilities that risked being merely clever and making them
meaningfully wise.

And both had an explicitly political point—almost, one feels, a
"message." Both Auden and Jarrell began as mandarins and ended as
liberals; the embrace of comedy, the folding-in of wit, the accept-
ance of artifice that Jarrell views so skeptically here is part of that
transition. Jarrell, in 1952, is still oddly uneasy with Auden's liberal-
ism, with the older poet's complacent acceptance of bourgeois
democracy, his love of "short" as opposed to long views, the "easi-
ness" of his forgiveness—as though some of the antiliberal mod-
ernist orthodoxy into which Jarrell had been indoctrinated by Tate
and Warren still clung to his mind. Eliot and Yeats, Lawrence and
Pound—Auden was, when Jarrell spoke, nearly the only unques-
tionable liberal among the unquestioned major poets. Much of Jar-
rell's complaint in these lectures still carries the sense, so powerful in
those years, that there is something wrong about this, too—that the
moderate liberal imagination was inadequate both to the austerities
of modernist art and to the horrors of modern history. In becoming
a liberal, one was no longer a poet. (In fact, Auden was not a liber-
al in quite this sense, and, as Jarrell says, he illogically makes Herod
in "For the Time Being" a "liberal" in order to mock liberal pieties.
But every Anglican mystic is a liberal in practice, since the love of
privacy and free thought is the most privileged of his feelings.)

Jarrell, in 1952, is still unsure of Auden's liberalism, his "vague hu-
manitarian mysticism," still inclined to believe that it acts as a bar-
rier to poetic consequence. But though Jarrell's own most humane
art would be neither vague nor mystical, it would achieve its great-
ness exactly through an embrace of Auden's "Euclidean city," the
small, lived experience of circles of friends and lovers, that "time be-
ing" in which we live and whose overestimation is at the heart of
what we mean by the liberal imagination. Auden, in his long poems

of the 1940s, travels the cosmos to come back to the dinner table, and this coming home (to a nostalgia for the past, to a wife encountered on the street) is also at the heart of the best poems that Jarrell would eventually write. That the liberal imagination need not be fatuous in art if it is willing to be funny, that a love of short views is no problem for a poet of the close at hand, that wit is the brevity of soul, its paraphrase and proof—these are all attitudes that, however excoriated as they may be at times by the lecturer in these pages, the two poets would eventually share. It does not, therefore, require too keen a wish for our heroes and fathers to spend the afterlife in perpetual peace to sense, in this agitated parting of the ways, intimations of a beautiful convergence.

Randall Jarrell on W. H. Auden

Introduction

[1]

During the spring of 1952, before an invited audience at Princeton, Randall Jarrell delivered six lectures on the poetry, prose, and career of W. H. Auden. These previously unpublished lectures are at once a passionate appreciation, a witty attack from an informed opponent, an important document of a major poet's reception, and a key to another poet's career. Randall Jarrell was reading Auden almost as soon as he was reading any modern poetry at all: he explains in one of these lectures that he discovered *Paid on Both Sides* in 1932, the year he turned eighteen. In the fall of that year Jarrell entered Vanderbilt University, where he encountered Robert Penn Warren (then a teaching assistant), Allen Tate, and John Crowe Ransom, Jarrell's early sponsors and mentors; while they were rereading Eliot and Donne (and Southern history and politics), Jarrell was reading and rereading Auden (and experimental psychology and psychoanalysis and Marxist theory—sometimes the same theorists Auden had read). Even in his studies of academic experimental psychology, Jarrell was—as he may have realized—making himself one of Auden's best-prepared interpreters: his particular interest, the Gestalt psychology of Wolfgang Köhler and Kurt Koffka, crops up among the diagrams in Auden's book-length poem *The Orators*.[1]

Jarrell began publishing poems in journals in 1934. He said later that he was never influenced by the Auden he admired most, the mysterious, dense, and intuitive poet of *Poems* (1930) and *Paid on Both Sides*.[2] Jarrell's early poems often sound instead like the Auden of *On This Island* (1935). This untitled poem (collected in Jarrell's 1942 volume *Blood from a Stranger*) takes from the Auden of that period its trimeters, its grammatical preferences (such as the omitted articles), and even one of Auden's favorite words, "lucky":

> When you and I were all,
> Time held his trembling hand,
> Fall's leaves lay long, the snows
> Were grave on wire and wand;
> Along the echoing ways
> Our steps were lucky on the stone;
> And, involved in our embrace,
> Man's intent and mercy lay
> Dazed through love's exacting day.[3]

Jarrell also imitated, with verve and accuracy, Auden's later imitations of popular songs:

> You're the can and I'm the salmon,
> You're the feathers, I'm the goose,
> You're the shell and I'm the oyster—
> Love me, leave me, I can't lose.[4]

Jarrell's "Over the florid capitals," with its diminishing candle, its "nightmare," and its "speechless cities of the night," is a pessimistic answer-poem directed at Auden's "September 1, 1939."[5] As Jarrell tried to put Marxist, psychoanalytic, and existentialist ideas into the increasingly discursive poems he wrote in the early 1940s (what William Pritchard calls, disparagingly, Jarrell's "political economy"

style), he found in Auden an essential resource for the long abstract
sentences he used:

> We who have possessed the world
> As efficiently as a new virus; who classified the races
> Species and cultures of the world as scrub
> To be cleared, stupidity to be liquidated, matter
> To be assimilated into the system of our destruction;
> Are finding how quickly the resistance of our hosts
> Is built up—can think, "Tomorrow we may be remembered
> As a technologist's nightmare."[6]

Jarrell's 1942 essay "The End of the Line" explains that "Modernist
poetry . . . is actually an extension of romanticism"; "Auden was so
influential" (in the 1930s) "because his poetry was the only novel
and successful reaction against modernism."[7] Yet Jarrell excoriated
other young poets who followed Auden too closely: one review
from 1940 called Frederick Prokosch "a sort of decerebrate Auden,
an Auden popularized for mass consumption."[8] In the decade to fol-
low (especially after he entered the Army in 1943) Jarrell would in-
vent another style entirely, devoted to realistic speech and interior-
ized characters—the virtues that, in Jarrell's view, Auden lacked.

Jarrell's apprenticeship as a poet informed his work as a critic.[9] In
a sensitive and detailed essay on the two poets' relations, Ian San-
som writes that "Jarrell's pre-eminence as a critic was based on his
articles about Auden and his notoriety as a reviewer derived from
his attacks on young Auden-influenced poets."[10] Sansom perhaps
claims too much (Jarrell attacked all sorts of poets, and published
long essays about Yeats, Housman, and modern poetry in general).
Yet Sansom does show how attention to Auden continued through-
out the younger poet's career. "I really know Auden's poetry pretty
well," Jarrell told Warren in 1935, promising an article on Auden for
Warren's *Southern Review*.[11] At Vanderbilt, Jarrell had tried to write
his master's thesis on Auden, switching to Housman when Donald
Davidson told him a living (and fairly young) poet made an inap-
propriate subject. Besides reviewing several of Auden's books as

they appeared, Jarrell published two long, much-noticed critical articles, "Changes of Attitude and Rhetoric in the Poetry of W. H. Auden" (*Southern Review*, autumn 1941) and "Freud to Paul: The Stages of Auden's Ideology" (*Partisan Review*, fall 1945). He wrote to Allen Tate in 1945, "I've been making many notes . . . for a book on Auden. . . . I'm going to make several articles out of different parts."[12] (All these writings became ingredients—in whole or in part—for the Princeton lectures.)

"Changes of Attitude" described the evolution of Auden's style, from the density of his earliest work to the public clarity of *Another Time*. Strongly preferring the former to the latter, Jarrell was articulating not only his reaction to one poet's work but his reservations about the public functions that many younger poets in America (especially those who shared Jarrell's left-wing views) wanted poetry to serve. Jarrell wrote, in one passage not incorporated into the later lectures:

> Auden has been successful in making his poetry more accessible; but the success has been entirely too expensive. Realizing that the best poetry of the twenties was too inaccessible, we can will our poetry into accessibility—but how much poetry will be left when we finish? Our political or humanitarian interests may make us wish to make our poetry accessible to large groups; it is better to try to make the groups accessible to the poetry, to translate the interests into political or humanitarian activity. . . . To write as good and plain a poem as you can, and to find it over the heads of most of your readers, is enough to make anyone cry. The typical solution of the twenties . . . and the typical solution of the political poetry of the thirties . . . were inadequate simplicities, absurd half-truths. . . . Auden's more appealing solution has worked out much better; it is too conscious, too thin, too merely rational; we should distrust it just as we distrust any Rational (or Rationalized) Method of Becoming a Saint. I am not going to try to tell the reader what the solution should be, but I can tell him where to find it: in the work of the next first-rate poet.[13]

Jarrell must have felt these pressures towards clarity, public communication, and political relevance with particular intensity, being himself attentive to politics and extraordinarily well read (not only in poems and novels and plays but in Freud and Marx, in Engels and Kardiner and Köhler). One can hear at the end of this influential essay not only a critic evaluating a major author but a young poet trying to decide where his own work should go.

"Freud to Paul" focuses not on Auden's style but on his ideas, taking (compared to "Changes") a more overtly hostile stance towards the Auden of the 1940s. The essay bears the marks of its wartime composition, both in its urgent tone and in its appalled reactions to (what it considers) Auden's repudiation of social action of any kind. (Auden himself would retreat, in the 1950s, from some of the views Jarrell attacked.)[14] Auden increasingly (Jarrell argues) let himself become witty, reactive, "secondary"; he relied too much on the conscious intellect: as a result Auden cut himself off from the real sources of aesthetic power, from his own unconscious preoccupations. Worse yet, Auden had become (if he was not always) someone to whom other people are not, or not sufficiently, real. It is no great leap from the Auden Jarrell portrays to the poet and critic of *Blood for a Stranger* and so many sharpened reviews, the Jarrell of 1937 through 1942, as portrayed by those who remembered him: intensely verbal, devoted to ideas, and sometimes oblivious to the feelings of other adults. Read in the context of Jarrell's other work, "Changes" and (even more so) "Freud to Paul" suggest that Jarrell saw in Auden's faults (or in the faults he identified with Auden) the temptations and flaws—both moral and aesthetic—Jarrell would himself have to work to avoid.

Readers of Jarrell see in these writings an Oedipal struggle or the anxiety of influence: readers of Auden remember them as attacks. Monroe Spears, in the early 1960s, found that Jarrell's essays had "done profound damage to Auden's reputation"; John Haffenden calls them "brilliantly destructive."[15] If these essays were the most stinging critique, and perhaps the most detailed readings, of Auden which had yet appeared in America, they were hardly the only ones. *Poems* (1930) attracted reviews from Morton Dauwen Zabel in *Poetry* and from Dudley Fitts in *Hound and Horn; Poems* (1934), notice from the *Nation*, the *New Republic* and the *New York Herald Tribune*.[16]

Nor were academic studies lacking: Cleanth Brooks took an extended example from Auden for a chapter of *Modern Poetry and the Tradition* (1939). The American professor James Southworth's *Sowing the Spring* appeared in 1940; its laudatory chapter on Auden acknowledged in his poetry "the prominence of an unconventional (the homosexual) theme."[17] Francis Scarfe published *Auden and After* in Britain in 1942; Richard Hoggart's book-length study appeared there in 1951. American poets who had admired Auden during the late 1930s continued to admire him in the 1940s, even if they did not know how to take his most recent works: Karl Shapiro (whose own verse included more than a touch of the Audenesque) claimed in his 1945 *Essay on Rime*: "The man whose impress on our rhetoric / Has for a decade dominated verse / In London, Sydney and New York is Auden."[18] While Jarrell's writings of the 1940s helped to shape Auden's American reputation, they were not alone, and they certainly could not kill that reputation (nor did they mean to do so). Jarrell seems to have meant those writings instead (to use a word he was still using then) as dialectical, showing how Auden's faults evolve out of his virtues, how one phase in his work led to the next.

Even as he deplored Auden's recent directions—and after he escaped Auden's obvious influences in the style of his own poetry—Jarrell remained fascinated by Auden's work as a whole and continued to plan a long critical study of him. The narrator in Jarrell's 1954 novel *Pictures from an Institution* "knows Auden by heart, practically."[19] Jarrell told Elisabeth Eisler in early 1949 "Mostly I've been writing prose about Auden, when I've written anything."[20] The one-page preface to *Poetry and the Age* (probably written in 1951 or 1952). explains, "I have written so much about Auden's poetry that the articles and lectures make two-thirds of a book; consequently they weren't included here."[21] It was in this mood, and with these plans, that Jarrell (having secured a leave from his regular job at the Woman's College of North Carolina in Greensboro) agreed to spend the academic year of 1951–52 at Princeton University. There he would give a series of lectures on Auden; these lectures might have provided the stimulus for him to complete and assemble that book.

[2]

The Princeton Seminars in Literary Criticism (later renamed the Christian Gauss Seminars) began in 1949 with a $30,000 grant from the Rockefeller Foundation; they invited prominent scholars in the literary humanities to campus for a set number of evening lectures (usually six) followed by discussions with an invited audience. Scholars were expected to attend one another's lectures throughout the year, though such attendance could not have been a requirement. Francis Fergusson, the Princeton English professor and scholar of theater, administered the seminars; in practice, R. P. Blackmur, head of Princeton's Creative Writing Program, had much to do with the invitations. The seminars were not open to the public and hence not publicized in student newspapers and alumni reports.[22] Fergusson's report to the president of the university details the lecturers for 1951–52: Herbert Read ("The Cult of Sincerity: Organic Form in English Poetry, Coleridge to Pound," October–November 1951), Father Pierre de Menasce ("On the Relative Independence of Thought from Language," November–December 1951), Americo Castro ("Man and the Humanities," February–March 1952), and Jarrell. Kenneth Burke also dropped by to give one seminar on Coleridge's "Ancient Mariner" in January.[23]

Jarrell's own seminars, collectively entitled "On the Poetry of W. H. Auden," took place on March 27, April 3 and 24, and May 1, 8, and 15. Fergusson's report describes them thus:

> Mr. Jarrel [sic] spent the year at Princeton teaching creative writing with Mr. Blackmur, and was a regular member of the Seminar Group all year. He presented a very thorough treatment of Auden's work and development as a writer. Mr. Jarrel writes and speaks with clarity and wit. What he had to say about Auden was of particular interest to those who themselves write verse.[24]

Jarrell held the title of "Resident Fellow in Creative Writing"; he received $3,500 for his teaching, and an additional $1,500 for his lectures on Auden.[25] The combination of duties was normal; other resident fellows during the 1940s and 1950s (some of them Gauss Seminar participants) included Joseph Frank, Leslie Fiedler, Robert Fitzgerald, and Delmore Schwartz.[26]

Jarrell's year at Princeton was neither as predictable, nor as productive, as he might have expected when he agreed to come. In July 1951, attending the Rocky Mountain Writers' Conference in Boulder, Colorado, he met Mary von Schrader; by the end of the conference, they had fallen in love. Randall soon asked his first wife, Mackie, for a divorce. Mary lived in California with her two young daughters; much of Randall's time and energy in Princeton went into letters to Mary, logistics for their visits, and plans for their marriage and later life together. In Princeton Jarrell resided at 14 Alexander Street (where T. S. Eliot lived while writing *The Cocktail Party*); the house belonged to the Princeton English professor Donald Stauffer, who was spending the year at Oxford.[27] Jarrell had arranged for these accommodations before he and Mackie split up; the house suited a couple more than a bachelor, and visitors were surprised by its disorder.

Randall's letters to Mary make 1951 and 1952 two of the most thoroughly documented years of the poet's life.[28] The letters concern the couple's travel plans; classical music (good and bad) on Princeton radio; Randall's visits to Greensboro and to Cambridge, Mass. (where he stayed with the Harvard literary scholar Herschel Baker and his family); Randall's Princeton companions and colleagues, in particular the difficult R. P. Blackmur and the friendlier John and Eileen Berryman; and a projected novel, *The Ladies*, on which Randall and Mary planned to collaborate. Most of the letters are simply love letters, describing and affirming the affections the pair felt for each other and tracing the gestures they made to show it, from nicknames and private jokes to a honeydew melon sent to Princeton with affectionate words carved on it. The letters contain several poems he would later publish (some, such as "The Lonely Man," set in Princeton) and several love poems, the most substantial of which ("If I could I would sing you to sleep" and "It is already late, my sister") were published posthumously.[29] Many of the letters

appear in *Randall Jarrell's Letters* (1985, 2002); those still unpublished
include at least one (perhaps fragmentary) serious poem never pub-
lished, "The God in the Chemistry Library":

In the library the cast of a statue
(The god the students do not recognize)
Thrusts aloft its serene and dirty face
Above the accustomed or indifferent eyes
Calm with the different drug of fact.
The stretched hand is sleek with grace
But broken—the armature shows through.
There is still grace, a saving in the hand?
There is no one here to ask: it is plaster
Or worse to those eyes, the rust and iron
Of its rude skeleton are plain.
Has knowledge then no need for grace?
No need, no need; the supple and empty hand
Has kept no blessing but its beauty.

Like other poems ("The School of Summer") and essays ("The Age
of Criticism") Jarrell wrote in the late 1940s and early 1950s, "The
God" reflects Jarrell's resistance to disciplinary specialization, which
he viewed as a menace to any art. He also complained about spe-
cialized academics in letters to Mary, writing sometime in the fall of
1951: "Everybody [at Princeton] has been *very* nice to me; and yet I
look at them, all critics and English professors and such, and give a
sort of impatient sigh and feel, 'That's not the *point!*' They're all so sat-
isfied with their world, even the ones that are most dissatisfied with
it and the world; even while they're not believing They Believe."

The letters provide only occasional insights into the structure
and argument of the lectures. Some exceptions prove the rule by
showing how much he wanted to avoid writing the lectures, or writ-
ing anything other than poetry and love letters. Sometime in fall
1951 Randall tells Mary, "I think Auden would forgive me anything
harsh I've ever said about him if he knew that I'd spend several pages
of a letter to *thee* copying out his poems. Or rather, he would until

he learned that every one was an *early* poem; then he'd want to kill me, poor thing. It must be *awful* to get steadily worse and worse."[30] One November letter reads "Oh, oh, *oh!* I don't like to write criticism, baby. Here I sit surrounded by wicked remarks about the last 3 parts of Williams' *Paterson*; but the worst part of it is, half of them are still in my head. Let's be Critics of Tomorrow, living in the House of Tomorrow, and just Grade poems: 'Paterson Part IV is a 6-B poem and gets a 72 on examination.' Or something." Jarrell planned to finish most of the lectures in the fall; he wrote in early October 1951: "I've worked fairly well, about half the time, on my Auden. . . . So all goes well like a marriage bell, as the poet says. Like hell it does—it's *dull*. I'm a poet, Mother, aren't I? I shouldn't be writing old *criticism*, should I?" In fact, the fall and winter of 1951 did produce famous and successful criticism, including "Some Lines from Whitman," "The Age of Criticism," and a long essay on William Carlos Williams, whose deadlines Jarrell worked hard to meet.

Those months did not, though, produce the rest of the lectures. Jarrell wrote on 8 or 9 February 1952: "This weekend I start on a couple of Auden articles—the undone half of my Auden lectures, that is. How I hope having made myself write 'The Age of Criticism' will carry over to making myself write the Auden! Surely the will, like Other Things, gets bigger with exercise."[31] He told Mary in January 1952 that writing critical prose "takes forever, such awful dandelion-like flourishes of will, such a black imminence of a deadline, before I can get myself going—and when I do I write pretty fast and enjoy it pretty much." Jarrell would continue to work on some of the lectures until almost the day he would give them. A letter dated 4 March 1952 explains that Randall has written "eleven pages on my next Auden lecture": "Part of my Auden was some comments (some quite funny, I think) on a bad poem named 'Spain 1937.' If you'd been there I'd have read them aloud to you." In April he wrote "I wish I could give up Auden-lecture-writing for Lent." Another letter, dated 10 April, says: "In the Golden Age *nobody* thought of writing lectures on Auden, and surely you and I are leftovers from it. Down with Auden. . . . Thank God I liked his last book better when I read it over for the fourth time. Even times I like it better, odd times I like it worse."[32]

By this point the lectures themselves had begun. Mary's last visit to Princeton coincided with some of those lectures (thus the absence of letters to Mary describing them). Mary did not attend the lectures during her spring visit—"my presence was kept a secret," she recalls; Mary and Randall did, however, visit New York together, where they "saw Hannah Arendt" and several operas.[33] Later lectures took place in between Randall's poetry readings in Mississippi, Iowa, and New York.[34] (He also gave a poetry reading for students, through Princeton's English Club.)[35] Jarrell's attitude toward his lectures, while he was giving them, included varying parts of pride, enthusiasm, exasperation, and fatigue. He improvised parts of at least some lectures in response to his audience, a tactic the seminars' format encouraged (and that explains the lectures' varying lengths). In April 1952 he wrote to John Crowe Ransom, "Giving six two-hour (written out beforehand) lectures on Auden is making me wish that Auden had never existed."[36] He wrote to Mary in a letter dated 24 April, "I worked fairly well today; I'spec by the end of tomorrow I'll have my fourth lecture almost done. Deliver my third tomorrow night, ending at ten." Earlier that day, he continues, "I wrote a cute sentence about a very effective sort of Henry James parody-style that Auden wrote one long piece in: 'Even the style is rocket-propelled James; the reader murmurs, his eyes widening: "Who would have thought the old man had so much blood in him?" ' "[37] The following night (after giving lecture 3) Randall told Mary: "My lecture was successful enough but Blackmur practically drove me crazy—in the discussion period he talked more than everybody else put together."[38] The same letter continues: "Worked pretty hard on the lectures today—won't it be wonderful when I'm through? I won't write a book on Auden for anything in the world; I'll make a long essay (for my second critical book) of the best stuff of mine on Auden that's already been published, and then I'll write an essay on *Paid on Both Sides*, and that'll be *that*."[39]

Besides Blackmur, Jarrell's audience included the composer Edward Cone, the poet and translator Robert Fitzgerald, Fergusson, and "an old German named Erich Kahler," a historian, social philosopher, and friend of Arendt.[40] The lectures struck Jarrell as enjoyable during their delivery and as well-received by the scholarly listeners, the often cantankerous Blackmur excepted. Of the 2 May lecture (lecture 4), Jarrell wrote: "I really felt so gay-serious, competent, and inspired while I talked, and was able to think of long elaborate sentences, lovely phrases, attractive informalities, etc.—so that the impromptu parts were better than the written ones."[41] He told Sister Bernetta Quinn on or around 6 May: "I'm almost all done with my Auden lectures and am *very* glad to be. Writing them and two articles took so much of my time that I didn't get much poetry written."[42]

By the end of the experience, Jarrell had lost—at least for the moment—his desire to write an entire book on Auden, though parts of the "Auden notebook" (described below) suggest that he considered the project again later on. He did, in any case, review Auden once more in 1955, and as late as 1957 he planned to incorporate writings on Auden into another book of his critical prose.[43] Manuscripts, typescripts, and notes now associated with the lectures include many plans and notes for the book. Though no one can prove the manuscripts of the lectures were *not* revised later, most of them show no evidence of it. The exceptions are texts printed here as lecture 4; Jarrell revised these with several inks, one of which makes revisions to turn a commentary on *Nones* (1951) into a review of *The Shield of Achilles* (1955).

Along with these manuscripts (described below) there survives what the Berg Collection calls Jarrell's "Auden notebook," apparently used between 1941 and 1953, with some pages torn out: Jarrell used the notebook for several critical projects, among them his projected book on Auden.[44] The first page reads, "Have book in two parts—Ideology and Poems? . . . Use that poem in *Harper's*—the anti-moral very late Auden having art frivolity and charming himself by attacking those boring moralists he's always been at the head of"; there follow notes for what became lecture 1.[45] The notebook contains conjectural tables of contents both for the Auden book and for *Poetry and the Age*: one table of contents, for a book to be called

Poets, lists several essays which ended up in the latter volume along with "3 Auden—one to be written." The next page considers "Auden and Others" as a book title, along with "Easy Modern Poets," "On Reading Widely," "The Difficulties of Criticism," "Auden and 18 Americans," "The English Rilke," and "Rereading." Another page includes a table of contents for a whole book on Auden: "Freud to Paul / Rhetoric / Long Poems / Best Poems / Spain / Nones (Yale Review)."[46] The reverse of this page includes other possible tables of contents, in Arabic and later Roman numerals: "1. Partisan Review article / I Freud to Paul / II The Great Gestalt / III [blank] / IV 2. First part of S[outhern] R[eview] article / V. 4. Auden's rhetoric—S. R. section + Age of Anxiety / VI 6. The First and Best / Early Auden + best Auden poems—new essay (& language of early Auden)." The same page contains the comment "as sure they'll be reading those poems (best in early) in 2 or 3 hundred years as still be reading Conrad or anything else."[47]

Auden chose not to attend Jarrell's lectures about him. He did, however, attend the earlier lectures by de Menasce, where Jarrell encountered him in person. Jarrell told Mary about one mid-November encounter: "Auden said almost nothing: his face has got so heavy and wrinkled and powerful and old, he's only 44, so that he looks like a (very disenchanted) lion, almost. He was awfully nice— he quite hurried over to me after the lecture and talked (he knew I was going to give my lectures on him—he said that before he knew they were on him he'd reply to someone 'Oh yes, I'm going to them') about my book, saying it was 'frightfully good.' "[48] After another lecture by de Menasce, Jarrell wrote to Sister Bernetta in December, "Auden came over to tell me that *The Seven-League Crutches* were 'frighteningly good.' This seemed awfully kind of him, considering what severe things I've said about his later work. He seems a model of disinterestedness about such things—several English writers have told me that they first read my poems because Auden recommended them."[49]

Against Jarrell's reactions to Auden, later critics have set Auden's (reported) reactions to Jarrell: one celebrated memoir has him telling Stephen Spender, "Jarrell is in love with me."[50] One need not

endorse that jocular claim to see how thoroughly and for how long
Jarrell considered what Auden had accomplished, what (wrong)
choices Auden had made, and what Jarrell in particular and the fu-
ture in general could admire in Auden's evolving work. It may be no
coincidence that while he was struggling with the rest of these lec-
tures, Jarrell was writing "The Age of Criticism": "the critic," he
writes there, "must get away from his self-as-self . . . without ever los-
ing the personal truth of judgment that his criticism springs from."[51]

If the lectures exhibit a unified argument (and readers will differ
as to whether they do), that argument concerns the "personal truth"
that gives durable poems their power. Jarrell insists that such truths
derive from the unconscious, from capacities none of us fully com-
prehend; in his view, Auden's later work had moved too far away
from those capacities, made too many concessions to the conscious
mind. Note cards in the Berg Collection include Jarrell's comment
(perhaps intended for "The Age of Criticism") that "criticisms are
works of art of an odd anomalous ancillary mode"; "it is often the
making into a work of art that distorts judgments." A reader unsym-
pathetic to Jarrell's own judgments might take his lectures on Auden
as an example: they are, at the least, works of art, with plenty of sen-
tences (including many written for the occasion) which describe the
processes of reading, writing, and judging poetry generally. (Auden
has, Jarrell concludes in lecture 4, "begun to get better again, and is
not laid away in that real graveyard of poets, My Own Style, going
on like a repeating decimal until the day someone drives a stake
through his heart.") A sympathetic reader might also see in Jarrell's
acceptances and rejections not only evidence of long, careful atten-
tion but the most intense and continued reading Auden had yet re-
ceived in America—a stimulus to judgments of our own.

[3]

Jarrell incorporated into these lectures parts of every piece of writ-
ing about Auden which he had published between 1941 and 1951;
along with his 1955 reviews of *The Shield of Achilles* (anticipated in part

by lecture 4), these lectures sum up his views about the stages of Auden's career. Readers who know "Changes in Attitude and Rhetoric" and "Freud to Paul" may find lectures 2 and 5 familiar; lectures 1, 4, and 6, by contrast, comprise material entirely (1, 6) or almost entirely (4) new to print. In assembling, editing, and annotating these six lectures from the surviving typescripts and handwritten texts, I have tried to approximate as nearly as possible the lectures Jarrell's Princeton audience actually heard; to create a clear and uncluttered reading experience, confining cruxes and alternate readings to notes; and to explain in those notes, as thoroughly as practicable, my own editorial decisions (and the textual support for them).

The six lectures and drafts and notes associated with them survive in nine numbered folders among Jarrell's papers at the Berg Collection of the New York Public Library; the first six are labeled as lectures no. 1 through 6. Folders 7 and 8 contain coherent material evidently written for the lectures, which I have placed in lectures 4 and 6, respectively, on the basis of internal evidence (explained in the notes to those lectures). Folder 9 consists of copious notes and short passages; these include:

many (and contradictory) one-page plans and outlines for the lectures or the projected book, at least some in the same thin, black ink used in the "Auden notebook," on pages perhaps torn from it;

five pages of notes on verse form, concentrating on the special requirements of accentual verse: one passage reads: "Auden probably best writer of A[ccentual] verse alive. . . . I have written great deal myself, and like ev[eryone] who writes [it] suffered from great ignorance about it . . . it is probably harder [to] write well, since such tremendous burden [of] choice [is] placed on writer, rules don't carry as much as in A[ccentual]-S[yllabic] verse";

two water-damaged pages on Auden and Isherwood's *The Ascent of F6*;

two pages of comments on Auden's *Collected Poetry* (1945);

one page of comments on (or a draft review of) Auden's *Another Time*;

two one-page fragments (on "For the Time Being" and "The Sea and the Mirror"), which I have integrated into lecture 6, for reasons explained in the notes to that lecture.

Some of the lecture manuscripts bear titles on their initial pages, but these titles are sometimes multiple and sometimes cancelled; other lectures read only "Lecture Two" or "Lecture Four" at the start (or a start) of an MS. I print the lectures without titles, giving the title markings (if any) in notes to each.

Jarrell's MSS and TSS often underline quotations rather than enclosing them in quotation marks; underlining in his MSS and TSS (corresponding to italics here) can represent either emphasis or quotation, while quotation marks can represent quotation, paraphrase (always indicated as such), or imagined speech by another speaker. Italics and quotation marks work the same way in the published "Changes" and "Freud to Paul," and in some of his other published criticism. Except as noted below, I preserve Jarrell's idiosyncratic choices here; for a work meant initially to be read aloud, they constitute, in effect, dynamic markings, analogous to those in sheet music. For titles of books, poems, and plays, on the other hand, I have converted Jarrell's idiosyncratic choices to standard usage (italics for book-length works, quote marks for shorter ones), since preserving Jarrell's choices there would create distractions with no clear benefit. Jarrell often used square brackets where most editors would require parentheses; sometimes the choice has a meaning (often brackets represent paraphrase or expansion of the phrase they follow, while parentheses represent added commentary). All phrases enclosed by square brackets in text are Jarrell's own except where brief additions are obviously editorial (e.g., [sic], [of], [the]). These other changes to Jarrell's manuscripts have been made to conform with Columbia University Press style: Arabic numerals for numbered poems (e.g., "10" or "poem 10" from Auden's *Poems* [1930]), where Jarrell used Roman ("X" or "poem X"); "gestalt" (but "Gestalt psychology") without italics, where Jarrell used italics.

Jarrell used several editions of Auden's poetry and plays in preparing his work. His usual sources, identifiable by his page number references, were *Collected Poetry* (New York: Random House, 1945) and *Poems* (New York: Random House, 1934). Both volumes are long out of print. My bibliographical notes to Jarrell's quotations refer to the standard, current editions of Auden's works that readers of this book are likely to use. These (all edited by Edward Mendelson) are: *The English Auden* (London: Faber and Faber, 1977), cited as *EA; Collected Poems* (New York: Vintage, 1976), cited as *CP; Plays and Other Dramatic Writings, 1928–1938*, by Auden and Christopher Isherwood (Princeton, N.J.: Princeton University Press, 1988), cited as *Plays;* and *Prose Volume 2: 1939–1948* (Princeton, N.J.: Princeton University Press, 2002), cited as *Prose2*. Where Jarrell's quotations differ both from *EA* and from *CP* I have checked them against *Collected Poetry* (1945), as reported in the notes; he sometimes misquotes from memory.

Mary Jarrell graciously provided the initial permissions that made this work possible. Hannah Brooks-Motl, my former student and a very capable critic herself, did much of the actual work of transcription. Jennifer Crewe has been a welcome, and patient, editor through all stages of the project; thanks also to Michael Haskell, Juree Sondker, and Clare Wellnitz at Columbia University Press for their patience, diligence, and expertise. Those at the Berg Collection have also been patient and helpful, as always. Macalester College provided the grants which allowed both Hannah's work and my own to go forward. For lecture 1, my colleague John Redmond tracked down some of the references; Edward Mendelson graciously, and from memory, tracked down the rest. For assistance with the remaining lectures, I thank Leslie Brisman, Nicholas Jenkins, J. D. McClatchy, Aidan Wasley, Joseph Frank, Demetri Debe, and the students and faculty of the English department at Macalester College; without the encouragement and the material support of Macalester College, these lectures would not have seen print. Susannah Gottlieb's generosity, patience, sharp eye, and sharper expertise, both in Auden and in German-language writing, caught and corrected a shocking number of errors; I am now enduringly grateful to her. I also thank Adam Gopnik for writing a preface to the book. Finally, thanks to Jessica Bennett, without whom not only this project, but much else, would be truly lost and without light.

Lecture 1

I magine a man on an island, a desert island. He loves poetry and has none; for years he has lived on nursery rhymes, "To a Wild-Fowl," the "Ode on a Grecian Urn." One morning, walking along the beach, he sees a packing box; he pries it open with a bone; there inside, in oil-cloth, is everything Auden ever wrote.[1]

He reads the poems, the plays, the criticism, over and over and over. He tires first of the plays: "I'd trade all three of them for one character," he grumbles, his dark face darkening. To a solitary man, what are plays written for a Left Book Club? to a man without a calendar, what are plays so dated that they seem occasional? A few choruses, a joke or two stick in his mind; the plays he forgets.

The criticism wears longer. Astonished at such individuality, cultivation, logic, the castaway exclaims, "Why, he's the finest dialectician since Kierkegaard!" But after a few weeks, throwing down a book and stamping on it, the man says furiously: "It was a black hour when first you learned to reason, you—*philosopher!* You've traded your soul to the devil for nineteen million generalizations."

Which sentence has so maddened him? That in which Auden decides that all Greek writers are essentially frivolous? That in which Auden states that all art is so frivolous that he himself prefers it to embody false beliefs, in order that the true may remain unsoiled? That in which—

It could be any of a thousand. The French call a typewriter a *machine for writing*; Auden, often, is a machine for generalizing. Many of his pieces of prose are dialectical constructions of startling elegance and airiness, meringues that tower like cumuli beside the goose-eggs of fact on which they were founded. For to Auden logic is, fundamentally, one more category of rhetoric, one more species of aesthetic organization, and he uses it almost as the Augustans used antithesis. (This was not true of the early Auden; then, when he felt something and wished to express it in prose, he made up sayings or parables which *New Verse*, and Geoffrey Grigson, and the younger inhabitants of the British Isles explained to people.)[2] Herbert Spencer defined a tragedy as a beautiful theory killed by an ugly fact: in this sense Auden is the least tragic of critics.[3] A critic must have, as Eliot has said, a very highly developed sense of fact; when he is told that his fact is a theoretical impossibility, he has no choice about replying: "but that doesn't keep it from existing." But Auden knows too many facts to care too much for any. A fact is for him a point of departure, a springboard for some sweeping or paradoxical or "exciting" generalization: the harder the fact, the higher he is flung into the thin cold air—the warm, bright, comfortable air—of theory. He has written a good deal—almost a great deal—of criticism, yet how many readers think of him as a serious critic? he is dazzling, enjoyable, and, finally, unconvincing. As a critic he is, in his own words, frivolous: to him a work of art is, usually, raw material for a generalization, a raw stimulus for an opportunity to astonish his readers, rather than what it needs to be—an object to be looked at steadily.

The castaway, then, leaves Auden's criticism for his poems. These are the poems of an extraordinary poet: that much is plain from the beginning. Or is it? are they, perhaps, the poems of several extraordinary poets? What kind of poet is it who says, however untruthfully, that the three main influences on his poetry are Langland, Dante, and Pope—when he also says, however truthfully, that the writers he "loves best and would wish most to resemble" are Edward Lear, Lewis Carroll, Ronald Firbank, and Beatrix Potter?[4] (He would need to add, today, J. R. [R.] Tolkien.) Auden has been attacked, at different times, as a Communist, a sentimental liberal, and a religious reactionary; the *New Masses* used to say that he was "really" a Fascist. Look into his book at random: there will be, on the first fifty or sixty pages, blues; Calypso songs; nursery rhymes; imitations of sagas, of Gilbert and Sullivan, of Henry James, of Greek choruses, of Lord Byron, Riding, Graves, Joyce, Skelton, Eliot, Yeats, Brecht, Perse, Rilke—many a reader must have murmured wistfully, "I just haven't read enough poetry to know *all* the poets Auden is influenced by." Graves says that Auden has never written an original line. Yet Graves's judgment is too absurd even to make us angry: Auden's originality is plainer than his influences, and he is, very obviously, one of the most original poets alive.[5] An ordinary poet is controlled by influences—he imitates, is possessed, against his own will or without his own knowledge; Auden consciously and actively *uses* influences, borrows them almost [as] he would borrow a word, a stanza-form, or a plot. Consequently he never gets what is essential in the poets he imitates, nor is what he borrows essential in him. For instance, no English poet has borrowed more from Rilke, on the surface; yet underneath Auden and Rilke are completely different, and Auden has not been influenced in any way by what anyone would call the real or essential Rilke. The affable familiar ghosts who possessed Yeats's wife announced to Yeats that they had "come to bring him metaphors for his poems"; all the poets of the world seem to be saying to Auden, "We have come to bring you techniques for your poems."[6] Technically, Auden is perhaps the most spectacularly and consciously accomplished poet since Swinburne; and this is rather disquieting to us—we know what we think of Swinburne.

Our castaway reads all the poems that Auden has ever written. After a few days, awed at their improbable variety, he begins to think of Auden as a Proteus upon whose back he can ride off in all directions. But he does not say about the poems, "here is God's plenty."[7] Here is far more than plenty; he looks about askance, and thinks it all some black or at least shady magic—particularly so because the magician keeps protesting, book in and book out, that it's all white, *white*. The castaway grumbles: "He moralizes me to the top of my bent."

Ordinarily a poet's *Come back and you will find me just the same* is the truth. Discover, young, that a hawk is better than a man, a stone better than a hawk, and you can spend the rest of a rich life saying so.[8] But Auden seems to be saying, *Come back in five years and you'll never know me*. Kafka called all that he had ever written *The Attempt to Escape from Father*; Auden could give what he has written the superficial title of *The Attempt to Escape from Auden*. Goethe called his own works "fragments of a great confession"; but Freud pointed to a bookcase full of them, collected for posterity, and remarked: "All that to hide himself from himself."[9] And one's ways of hiding from oneself are, in a sense, the most personal things one has; all those masks one wears so as not to recognize oneself in the mirror have, just at the back of the strangeness, the same hollows for the same head.

Auden's poems, the stages of his poetry, look extraordinarily different; but as the reader gets to know them well enough, thinks about them hard enough, it seems to him that he can see how and why they changed as they did—can see, even, what was constant underneath all the changes. Certainly that imaginary reader, the castaway, will think this; as I think about him, it more and more seems to me that, when the rescuers came for him, he was beginning to write a book about Auden in the sand, and had got as far as this first paragraph—this first Audenesque paragraph—about Auden's poetry:

It is a city many times rebuilt, and many times destroyed: the inhabitants starch old evening shirts for seances to which they once came blue with woad; level after level—flung down by welcomed catastrophes, burnt down by the unrepentant inhabitants, but rebuilt, always higher and flimsier than before—level after level looms from the midst of the tropical growths which, at some earlier epoch, were introduced into the conservatories of the city as potted plants. One hates to see the city's last improbable stages—half scaffolding and half rubble, grey with great stucco churches full of fetishes—one hates to see all that, a wonder of desolation, dismissed by the innocently young as a Hollywood set, or adored by the innocently religious as the City of God.[10]

The rescuers lead the man away. The castaway isn't troubled by having to leave behind those sentences in the sand; he knows them by heart. And I like to think that the rescuers hand him, as soon as they get him and his packing case safely aboard the boat, a copy of Auden's last book of poems. I imagine that the castaway has worked out for his book a long complicated analysis of Auden's development—this is particularly easy for me to imagine, since I have done so myself—have printed the analysis in *Partisan Review*, even—and could keep you here till midnight, and tomorrow midnight, and midnight a fortnight hence, describing Stage I and Stage II and Stage III.[11] Our castaway would surely cry out in delight, after his first look at Auden's new book: "Stage IV! Stage IV! Oh, give me some paper, hand me a pencil!" I see him disappearing into a cabin, his lips moving as if to say, "All changed, changed utterly!" And let's leave him there in the cabin: that castaway is an outworn conceit; let us talk about Auden's new book just as though you and I weren't castaways, but were—I don't know what—professors, let's say.[12]

Auden's earliest work, taken as a whole, has far more effect than any selection of the best poems from it—readers will usually think of this as a fault, but there is a good and unusual reason for it. *Poems* and *Paid on Both Sides* have implicit in them a picture of a world, a description and valuing of our existence, that are different in a number of ways from any we are accustomed to in earlier works of art—and even the mediocre poems usually supply us with essential elements of the pictures or with essential principles for organizing them. The world of the poems is consistently different from the "world of everyday reality," just as a scientific construct is different from the system it summarizes; it has to be: it is the differentness of the poems, all that is exaggerated or disregarded in them, that says to the reader, "this is what your world 'really' is." The world of these

poems is supposed to be a sort of map or vector-diagram of the be-
haviors and causes of things in our everyday world; but, since the
poems are poems, their world is a sort of empathy- or sympathy-
map, designed primarily to make us feel, and only secondarily to
make us understand, all these processes. As long as the right stress-
es and strains are set up in us, as long as we see the proper doom
over our heads whenever we stare into the proper mirror, Auden
does not worry much about our logical, prosaic, conscious under-
standing of the whole system; this can come later—or, if we don't
have the wit, industry, or inclination to work it out, we have still lost
the less important thing, he plainly feels.[13] My metaphors for the
world of Auden's early poems may sound surprisingly or distress-
ingly scientific, but Auden's view of things in those days depended
almost entirely on the sciences or pseudo-sciences, and hardly at all
on any of the Higher Religions. After all, he was (to quote him) "son
of a nurse and doctor, loaned a dream," and the dream was, to be-
gin with, one of being a mining-engineer, and then changed into a
psychological one, influenced by psychologists who resembled
Köhler or Lashley less than they resembled D. H. Lawrence's idea
of a *real scientist*; Auden had specialized in biology at the school he
went to, and had gone to Oxford on a scholarship in the natural sci-
ences; he was only twenty-two, twenty-three, twenty-four when he
wrote these poems.[14] But—let me hasten to add—he came from a
very Church of England family, was sure that—to quote him—"any
Prot / Will only squat / Instead of kneeling," loved to play hymn
tunes on the piano, and was already manifesting some of the ten-
dencies that made Isherwood later say of him, "If Wystan had his
way he'd make our plays nothing but choruses of angels."[15] (And, as
a matter of fact, the first semidramatic piece that Auden wrote with-
out Isherwood *was* an oratorio about the birth of Christ.) Trotsky
said about Celine that he was a man ripe for fascism, and Auden was
always a man ripe for religion; a system of ethics yearning for its
own teleological suspension.[16]

   The world of Auden's early poems—if one presents it as simply as
possible, in a diagram—is made up of three overlapping processes,
or fields. These processes are essentially similar, so much so that al-

most anything in one has its analogue in the other two: often a poem will develop or explain something in process A mainly in terms of its analogues in B or C. The small, central, primary process is that of ontogeny, of individual growth, of moral development; the largest and most removed process—removed in both time and space—is that of evolutionary development, of phylogeny. This ontogeny recapitulates phylogeny, as you would suppose; but so does what comes in between[:] the historical process (and its contemporary aspect, the "economic situation") which ranks between the other two, so far as size and importance are concerned. Each of these processes is made to recapitulate the other with astonishing faithfulness (it is just as though you were listening to Freud speculating about what specific event in the history of the race is responsible for the "period of sexual latency" from five to eleven). Auden will take exactly the same attitude, a very disapproving moral one (for, just as Richard III was born with a fine set of teeth, Auden was born with a fine set of morals)—Auden will take exactly the same disapproving attitude toward the species refusing to evolve, the country unwilling or unable to modernize its industry, that he takes toward the boy who stays home and clings to his mother. All have made the great refusal, and are—naturally and inevitably—condemned by this particular universe and its poet.

These three processes resemble each other so closely because the same principle of organization, the same polar force, is responsible for everything that happens in them; this principle, in early Auden, corresponds to gravitation in Newtonian dynamics, or to polarity in electronics. Everything in the universe is change, but all change is of two directly contradictory sorts: *Change Away From* and *Change Back To*. The first is Change +, good change, the second is Change −, bad change. The first is Development or Growth or Evolution, and is *the* principle of good in this universe of Auden's early poems; the second is Regression, in all its hideous shapes of Disease, Neurosis, Decadence, and Love. Probably that last word made my hearers jump; but this is one of the early Auden's firmest beliefs: that love is, first of all and last of all, a form of ontogenetic regression or backwardness, from which the individual, if he is to develop, must be "weaned at last to independent delight."[17] (This last phrase is a quotation from one of the best and most carefully worked out of Auden's early poems.) The *We must love one another or die* of Auden's middle period had developed out of the earlier, odder motto, *If we love one another, we die;* but the original *love* is the concrete, surprising Eros of case histories, the later *love* is the abstract, acceptable, ethereal Agape of speeches and sermons. Auden's position, then, could be expressed in Cromwell's words, *Not what they want, but what is good for them;* the two *never* coincide. This is Puritanical of course; but the early Auden is an oddly Puritanical Freudian, as is the superego. But once or twice in the early poems another sort of great generalized, inhuman Love is *mentioned*, and treated not as individual regression but as a sort of Lucretian Venus, an immanent urge (or as Hardy would say, Immanent Will) working through us, its unsatisfactory, ephemeral, willingly discarded instruments; in his *Collected Poems*, fifteen years later, Auden rather flippantly calls one of these poems *Venus Will Now Say a Few Words.*[18] "Venus" assures the lover, the loved one, relaxing in his "darling's arms like a stone," that

> joy is mine not yours—to have come so far,
> Whose cleverest invention was lately fur;
> Lizards my best once who took years to breed,
> Could not control the temperature of blood.
> To reach that shape for your face to assume,
> Pleasure to many and despair to some,
> I shifted ranges, lived epochs handicapped
> By climate, wars, or what the young men kept,
> Modified theories on the types of dross,
> Altered desire and history of dress.[19]

Another poem (10 in *Poems*, "Too Dear, Too Vague" in *Collected Poems*) distinguishes sharply between this Love and the love in which it is momentarily and unsatisfactorily incarnate, the individual love which begins as a process, but which "by ambition / Of definition / Suffers partition," and which ends in regression, a partial static success ("success / Views from the rail / Of land and happiness," as Auden phrases it), or else ends in an equally static failure, "The shutting of a door / The tightening jaw / A conscious sorrow." But the great Love, Love with a capital letter, "is not there / Love has moved to another chair."[20] *This* chair holds the being—it is hard not to give him some such title as the Virtuous Developer—who knows that love is *really* a Something Outside Us Working for Change, if I may parody Arnold's phrase. This true Developer realizes that he himself is a temporary, necessarily discarded instrument; cares only for the development working its way through and beyond him; and rejects with good grace that success and happiness in which the others hoped to rest. Consequently the Developer (the tone of the poem's ending is grim, approving, and heroic, almost that of Housman's army of mercenaries who died and "saved the sum of things for pay")—consequently the Developer "designs his own unhappiness / Foretells his own death and is faithless."[21] Nothing could be further from the way in which the ordinary lover is treated; *he* is usually tangled somewhere in a dismaying cluster of neurosis, perversion, economic-social seduction, general weakness, "dishonored portraits," "manors mortgaged / To pay for love," and so forth.[22]

Auden was thoroughly familiar with the Freudian view of a sexuality developing through stages, each of which has an organic localization or lack of localization reminiscent of some animal form of sexuality (Freud makes it plain that he thinks of this development as a recapitulation of the evolutionary development of the species); to remain fixed in any stage but the final genital, heterosexual stage is a kind of arrest or defeat—we are successful only when we reach the stage which is the goal of the whole process, and in difficult circumstances we may regress from it to an earlier, more primitive level. To have accepted this view without change or qualification would have been dissatisfying to Auden—would have been, pretty decidedly, to warm a snake in his bosom; yet his whole way of looking at things was so thoroughly psychoanalytic and evolutionary that he was required to accept this along with the rest. So Auden— the process is like dream-work, with the censor distorting things just enough to make the dream acceptable to it—devised the remarkably ingenious solution of accepting the whole set of stages, the whole ladder of sexual development, as *something to be developed out of*. We are truly successful only when we have left the ladder altogether, when we have been—as Auden says—"weaned at last to independent delight." But, till then, all the climbers are equal, since anybody anywhere on the ladder has met with a kind of defeat or arrest, is stranded in some stage that is fixation or regression as compared to this higher goal of true development, "independent delight." (Heterosexuality is accepted as little as homosexuality for—of course—both of these, *any* kind of sexuality, has been pushed out of sight by Authority during the child's whole development.) Auden is as vague about "independent delight," this last transcendental stage—almost no one in the poems attains it—as Marx is about things after-the-state-has-withered-away: what does one know about such things, stuck here on the ladder far below, except that they are going to be *different*?

Never but once (and this is some years later, in the poem that begins "The earth turns over, our side feels the cold"—and entitled in the *Collected Poems*, "Through the Looking-Glass") does Auden accept this Freudian view of our development without qualification, and regard his own stage of development as perhaps unsatisfactory or partial, as something it would be possible or even desirable to develop out of.[23] This poem is moving in its troubled sincerity; in it Auden accepts what then seems to him a disadvantage, a guilt or lack, as something that is special to himself, and not necessarily true for everybody; for once the "normal" has no quotation marks around it, and is not treated as—so to speak—one more coordinate subdivision of the abnormal. For once Auden does not say, *Each of us is alone forever, and he may as well get used to it;* instead he remembers the family in which he wasn't alone, and longingly speculates on whether he won't somehow, sometime in the future, be able to return to that togetherness.[24]

In early Auden everything is a process. Any kind of continued conservative existence, of static survival, of eternal object, is considered to be impossible—anything that resembles any of these is actually decadence, or insidious regression. There is—so to speak—a high negative rate of interest on everything in this world: the heaviest depositor, returning to his savings account after a few years, finds the teller's cage full of men waiting to attach his furniture—he has buried his talent in that bank too long. The best motto one can find for Auden's early poetry is, as I have said, Goethe's "What you have inherited from your fathers, you must earn in order to possess."[25] But Auden has astonishingly exaggerated the principle. (He reminds me of that disciple of Heraclitus who was so much in love with his master's saying, *We never step twice into the same river*, that he logically and methodically figured out, and no doubt, published in the *Hellenic Journal of Ontology*, that we never step *once* into the same river, since the water that washes our ankles is yards past us by the time we get in up to our knees.) What we have inherited from our fathers, Auden says, we *cannot* possess—cannot, that is, without becoming epigonic, decadent successor-states. "Then cannot mean to now," Auden writes with laconic force.[26] What was right for the father then is necessarily wrong for the son now; and the only tutelary authority the son can find, in his hunt for a sponsor for his new Way is that Uncle (with his slightly protruding eyes, now brown, now blue, now a "terrifying sea-green") who was the aberrant failure of the last generation.[27] It is no wonder that, when Auden finally did become able to accept God the Father, it was God the Wholly Other, all of whose relationships with us are *absurd, beyond* morality, the God of Kierkegaard and Barth and the neo-Calvinists—a very Uncleish sort of God, if one may speak of Him in the terms of *The Orators*. The demands on us of true morality, of Growth, are always new and unconditioned and surprising, and it is the ordinary demands of ordinary morality that are the greatest obstacle to *truly* moral behavior, since they try to confine us in those old ruts of behavior, good then, for others, evil now for us.

The early poem that gives the most thorough and systematic picture of the development of the individual, as Auden saw it then, is "Easter 1929." I will first make a kind of summary paraphrase of it and then read you the poem.[28]

The foetus, warm and happy in the mother's womb, one with the mother, is torn catastrophically from her; now even she (and, certainly, everything else, *always*) is alien, is cold and dry and thin with differentness. The child's thoughts in the daytime, his dreams at night, are swollen with his awareness of others, his fear of others: even a part of himself is alien, an enemy—he is alone in his separate flesh. He tries to forgive others for their alienness, for all that they do that thwarts and hurts him—they and their world, no part of his dream, are always stubbornly against his wish—unable, even if they wanted to, to satisfy him always, to be what he would choose for them to be. He tries to forgive, but essentially he is unforgiving, and underneath its love of others his body stubbornly loves death, that image of the womb it wishes to return to, that image of the inanimate state that preceded life. It is necessary for him to change, but he does so against his will; in each new stage of change, while—resisting—he is drawn irresistibly on to the next stage, he uneasily and miserably wishes to stay where he is, or to return to the last stage, he finds happiness only in a return to that simpler state, that "home," that "place / Where no tax is levied for being there," which demands of him always *less* than he is able to give.[29] (In these first few lines of "Easter 1929" Auden has introduced—as the hearer will see from my summary—birth trauma, infantile aggression, the superego, the primacy of aggression over Eros, the death wish, Freudian stages of sexual development, repetition compulsion, regression, the timelessness of the unconscious, and several other pieces of psychoanalytic doctrine.)

Sometimes—the poem goes on—for an instant of happiness, of aesthetic acceptance, he can love his own life for what it is; he can actually identify his own process of change with that of the world, can feel it as power and freshness, but then, always, he is reminded of his separateness, thrown back into his isolated self, by coming to "where solitary man sat weeping on a bench, / Hanging his head down, with his mouth distorted, / Helpless and ugly as an embryo chicken." This last image is too immediately effective to need any comment, but one could say about it this: The embryo chicken is so ugly and pathetic because it is a permanent state, a preserved cross-section of what should be a changing process. This Becoming ludicrously stopped in mid-air, in grotesque Being, reminds the individual that any state he has attained, even a successful one, is an ugly failure when permanent. This objective isolation of the organism reminds it that its feeling of oneness with the world, of power and success, is only an illusion. The individual is reminded of all those others "whose death / Is necessary condition of the season's setting forth"—of his own eventual failure and death. The whole process seems to him (in his exhausted despair) one that is hopeless for the individual, that leads only to death; no state of being is intrinsically good, final, but is only a way-station, something to be left, changed out of; the shower of rain that (in Auden's delicate pathetic fallacy) "fell willing into grass and closed the day," makes any choice seem to the individual "a necessary error." Nature itself is made to wish for death, for sleep, just as he does. Everything is determined—the individual has no choice, yet his choice seems to him, always, the wrong one.

So, essentially and finally insecure, he tries to find security in the otherness outside himself, in love; but love itself is insecure, always gives him less than he needs or expects, so that he doesn't know whether—[30]

> He knows not if it be seed in time to display
> Luxuriantly in a wonderful fructification
> Or whether it be but a degenerate remnant
> Of something immense in the past but now
> Surviving only as the infectiousness of disease
> Or in the malicious caricature of drunkenness;
> Its end glossed over by the careless but known long
> To finer perception of the mad and ill.

Man's love is made like man himself, a transitional animal at an unfortunate evolutionary stage, too early or too late. He loves what he hopes will last, something final and unchanging; an[d] it changes and is gone, just as he changes; and he mourns it and himself, wishing both what they were. The soul must be *weaned*—the metaphor is partly Freudian—the soul must be *weaned* to *independent delight*, must accept itself and its separation from others, instead of desperately trying to insist that the others are not "really" other, but are joined to it by love. Yet even if the cycle of its development leads it to this accepting fulfillment, to "independent delight," the fall and winter of the cycle are coming, bringing the death that has always been consciously or unconsciously wished for, bringing the demand that any individual good be transcended, that any individual success fail and die and be forgotten underground, there where the new potential life lies waiting to replace it. Most of *this* last is not Freudian at all, of course, but an unusually plausible-feeling dialectical evolution of a queer neo-Hegelian sort; the orthodox Freudianism earlier in the poem has never, I think, been more convincingly stated, been made more accessible to direct feeling. I will read the poem, a fairly long one, and let you hear for yourself.[31]

Lecture 2

In 1930 Auden was twenty-three. He and the friends with whom he identified himself were unwilling to accept the values and authority of their own society, that late-capitalist culture which, condemned by Marx, explained by Freud, and despaired of by no end of people, was still the only culture there to be accepted. Since he and his friends had rejected that established order of things, it was necessary to make for themselves a new one: they went hunting for an Authority to take the place of the one they had revolted against. Auden synthesized for them an order all their own. There were so few of them that he could consider individual interests and dislikes, and he considered most of all one thoroughly individual set of them, Wystan Auden's. (He could feel a certain freedom in his work, since it was a subsistent and not an existent order that he was creating.) He got the materials for his new order from several obvious and several surprisingly unobvious sources: (1) Marx. (2) Freud and Groddeck and Homer Lane: the risky, sometimes unscientific, fertile and imaginative side of modern psychology.[1] (3) The sciences, biology particularly: these seemed available to him because they had been only partially assimilated by capitalist culture, or else appeared incapable of being corrupted by it. (In those times no one, not Stalin nor Lysenko himself, knew enough to despise capitalist genetics.)[2] (4) All sorts of boyish sources of values: flying, polar exploration, mountain climbing, fighting, the "thrilling" side of science, public school life, sports, big-scale practical jokes, the "spies' career," and so forth. (5) Homosexuality: if the ordinary sexual values are rejected as negative and bourgeois, this can be accepted as a source of positive revolutionary values. (6) A cluster of related sources: the folk, the blood, intuition, D. H. Lawrence, fairy-tales, mysticism, parables—the young Auden loved parables as much as the older Auden loves neo-Hegelian, Kierkegaardian logical demonstrations. (The dialectical performance finally replaced the practical joke as a method of demonstrating against society, but it retained some of the arbitrary virtuosity of its predecessor.)

Auden was able to set up a We with whom to identify himself—rejection loves company—in opposition to the "legions of cruel inquisitive They," the Enemy.[3] Neither We nor They are the comparatively simple, clear, and distinct entities one finds in political or economic analyses, but are great conglomerations of heterogeneous elements: Auden was interested in establishing a dichotomy in which one side would get all the worst of it, and he wanted this *all the worst* to be as complete as possible, to cover everything from imperialism to underlining words in letters. A reader could be indifferent to some or most of Their bad qualities, but They were given so many that at some point, Auden hoped, the last man would break down and reject Them as Auden did. Auden wanted a total war, a total victory; he did not make the political mistake of taking over a clear limited position and leaving to the Enemy everything else. (This was Art, not politics—but everybody concerned was confused at times.) Auden's aptitude for giving everything he liked to Us, everything he disliked to Them, was sometimes clever and sometimes far-fetched, but sometimes sheer self-indulgence: if Auden had once disliked a relative with a bearskin rug in his parlor, then all over Greenland poor Eskimos went out in kayaks to satisfy Their insensate passion for polar bear rugs. (But this We-They system is

plainest in *The Orators; Paid on Both Sides* and the earlier poems, for-
tunately, are not systematic and revolutionary in this way.)

Auden began: The death of the old order is inevitable. It is al-
ready economically, morally, and intellectually bankrupt; We are
the Future, They are the Past. (Naturally the reader will side with
Us and that perpetual winner, the Future.) Auden derived most of
this from Marxism, but he was never at any time a thoroughgoing
Marxist—it would have meant giving up too much to the enemy.
He kept all sorts of things a Marxist rejects, and some of the doc-
trines he valued most were in direct contradiction to his Marxism.
At the ultimate compulsive level of belief most of his Marxism al-
ways disappeared; later during the 1930s it disappeared from any
level. His psychoanalytical, vaguely medical convictions were so
much more important to Auden—"son of a nurse and doctor, loaned
a dream"—that the fables he may have wished to make Marxist al-
ways turned out Freudian.[4] But Marxism as a source of energy, of vi-
olence, helped to counteract the sentimental and idealistic moral-
ism, the reliance on a finally reliable Love from the Machine, that
were endemic in Auden.

Obviously They represented business, industrialism, exploitation—
and worse than that, a failing business, an industrialism whose ma-
chines were already beginning to rust. Auden had seen what hap-
pened in England during what amounted to a long depression, and he
made a romantic and effective extension of this into an actual break-
down of the whole machinery, a Wells-ish state where industry and
commerce and transportation have gone to pieces, where the ships lie
"long high and dry," where no one goes "further than railhead or the
ends of piers," where the professional traveler "asked at the fireside . . .
is dumb."[5] The finest of these poems is 25 in *Poems;* history before the
event, one's susceptible and extravagant heart tells one. Here Auden
found a symbol whose variants were obsessive for him: *grass-grown pit-
bank, abandoned seam, the silted harbors, derelict works*—these, and the wires
that carry nothing, the rails over which no one comes, were poignant
to Auden, a boy who wanted to be a mining engineer, who "Loved a
pumping-engine, / Thought it every bit as / Beautiful as you."[6] The
thought of those "beautiful machines that never talked / But let the

small boy worship them," abandoned and rusting in the wet country-side—the early Auden sees even his machines in rural surroundings—was now and then, perhaps, as influential as more commonplace political and humanitarian considerations.[7]

Auden related science to Marxism in a way that is unexpected but perfectly orthodox [i.e., you can find a text for it in Marx, Engels, or Lenin]. Lenin says somewhere that in the most general sense Marxism is a theory of evolution.[8] Certainly Freud thought of psychoanalytical theory as, from one point of view, an extension of evolutionary biology. Auden quite consciously made these connections: evolution, as a source both of insight and of image, is just behind all his earliest poems. This, along with his unexpected countryishness—he had begun to write poetry by imitating Hardy and Edward Thomas—explains his endless procession of birds and beasts, symbols few of these poems are without. Number 4 in *Poems* ("Venus Will Now Say a Few Words" in the *Collected Poetry*) is nothing but an account of evolution, by some neo-Hardyish Immanent Will behind it, and a rather Marxist extension of it into man's history and everyday life. The critical points where quantity changes into quality, the Hegelian dialectic, what Kenneth Burke calls neo-Malthusian limits—all these are plain in the poem.[9]

There are many examples of this coalition of Marxism and biology; the prettiest example, though by no means the best poem, is 9 in *Poems*, with its refrain, "Here am I, here are you: / But what does it mean? What are we going to do?"[10] The *I* of the poem is supposed to be anonymous and typical, a lay-figure of late capitalism; he has not kept even the dignity of rhetoric, but speaks in a style that is a blank parody of popular songs. He has arrived at the end of his own blind alley with a wife, a car, a mother-fixation, a vacation, and no use for any of them. All he can make himself ask for is some fresh tea, some rugs—this to remind you of Auden's favorite view of capitalism: a society where everyone is sick. Even the instincts of this particular Ego have broken down—he doesn't want to go to bed with Honey, all the wires to the base in his spine are severed. The poem develops in this way up to the next-to-the-last stanza:

In my veins there is a wish,
And a memory of fish:
When I lie crying on the floor,
It says, "You've often done this before."

This "wish" in the blood is the evolutionary will, the blind urge of
the species to assimilate the universe. He remembers the species of
fish which at a similar impasse, a similar critical point, changed over
to land and a new form of being. Here for the millionth time—the
racial memory tells the weeping individual—is the place where the
contradiction has to be resolved; where the old answer, useless now,
has to be transcended; where the last of the quantitative changes is
over, where the qualitative leap has to occur. The individual re-
members all these critical points because he is the product of them.
And the individual, in the last stanza, is given a complete doom:

A bird used to visit this shore:
It isn't going to come any more.
I've come a very long way to prove
No land, no water, and no love.
Here am I, here are you:
But what does it mean? What are we going to do?

His bankruptcy and liquidation are taken as inevitable for the spe-
cies, a necessary mode of progression; the destructive interregnum
between the old form and the new is inescapable, as old as life. . . .
In the war between Us and the Enemy the strategic value of Auden's
joining of Marxism and evolution, his constant shifting of terms out
of one sphere into the other, is this: the reader will tend to accept
the political and economic changes Auden desires—their form,
even—as themselves inevitable, something it is as ludicrous or pa-
thetic to resist as it would be to resist evolution.

When compared to the folkish Us, They are complicated and
subtle. Calling them this is neither praise nor description, but
blame: subtlety and complication are to the early Auden some of
the worst of sins, and nothing appeals to him, complicated and

subtle creature that he is, like simplicity. He tells the embryo that "almost all / Shall be as subtle when you are as tall: / Yet clearly in that 'almost' all his hope" lies; that a few people will have grown simpler is all that we can hope for from the future.[11] (Later on Auden learned to accept his own state with despairing resignation, and in the *Collected Poetry* he changed an earlier poem's accusing "subtle useless faces" to "sad and useless faces.")[12] Meanwhile We go on struggling with Them, Alexandrians compiling a barren encyclopedia. They are scholarly, trained, and introspective observers; We have the raw insight and natural certainty of the naive, of Christ's children, of fools, of the third sons in fairy tales.

They are aridly commercial, financial, distributive; We represent real production, the soil. They are bourgeois-respectable or perverted; We are folk-simple or else consciously Bohemian, Dada even, so as to break up Their system and morale—there is in Us more than a suggestion of the prodigal son, of rebirth through sin. They represent the sterile city, We the fertile country; I want to emphasize this, the surprisingly rural character of so many of Auden's earliest poems, because so far as I know everyone has emphasized the opposite. They are owners, executives, white-collar workers, idlers—those who neither "make" nor "do"; We are scientists, explorers, farmers, manual laborers, aviators, conspirators—all the real makers and doers. Auden gets science over on Our side by his constant use of it both for insight and images, by his admiring preoccupation with the adventurous and imaginative side of it; he leaves to Them only the "decadent complexity" of Jeans or "psychological" economics.[13]

All this is likely to seem a lot too good to be true; the reader, unless he is an unusually virtuous one, is likely to nourish a perverse seed of liking for Them, bad as They are. When one of Them is looked down on for doing something "with the typical assurance of the non-airman"—hideous substantive!—it is hard for me not to grit my teeth, give up all the airplanes in my life, and decide that I'm a non-airman, too.[14]

Since Auden was forced to reject Tradition, he set up a new tradition formed of the available elements (available because rejected, neglected, or misrepresented) of the old. There are hundreds of examples of this process—particularly when it comes to appropriating old writers as Our ancestors; the process was necessary partly to reassure Auden, but partly to reassure his readers, who otherwise would have had to reject Our position because accepting it necessitated rejecting too much else. One can see the workings of this process in the form of Auden's early poems, even: in all the Anglo-Saxon imitation; the Skeltonics; the Hopkins accentual verse, alliteration, assonance, consonance; the Owen rhymes; the use of the fairy story, parable, ballad, popular song—the folk tradition They have rejected or collected in Childs.[15] Thus Auden selected his own ancestors, made from the disliked or misprized his own tradition.

In *The Orators* Auden shows, by means of the ordinary Mendelian inheritance chart, that one's "true ancestor" may be neither a father nor a mother, but an uncle.[16] (His true ancestor wasn't the Tradition, but the particular elements of it most like himself.) This concept was extremely useful to Auden in (a) family, (b) religious, and (c) political relations. (a) By this means he acquired a novel and active type of family relationship to set up against the ordinary family and its passive, all too feminine inertia. (b) God could be addressed and thought of as Uncle instead of as Father. God the Uncle will help revolutionary Us as naturally and appropriately as God the Father helps His legitimate and conservative sons, the Enemy. This Uncle has, in *The Orators*, a Christlike sacrificial-hero representative on earth, who is surrounded with a great deal of early-Christian, secret-service paraphernalia. This hero is confused or identified with (c) the political leader, a notably unpolitical kind of fantasy-Hitler, who seems to have strayed into politics with his observers only because he lives in an unreligious age. There is hardly more real politics in early Auden than in G. A. Henty; what one gets is mostly religion, hero-worship, and Adventure, combined with the odd Lawrence-Nazi folk-mysticism that serves as a false front for the actual politics behind it, which Auden doesn't treat.[17] There is a sheltered but insecure, very *young* feeling to it all: this Leader seems to pick his disciples not among fisherfolk but among public school boys on their summer vacation.

When Auden occasionally prays to this Uncle he asks in blunt definite language for definite things. It is a personal, concrete affair. In the poetry of his middle period Auden is always praying or exhorting, but he prays to some abstract, eclectic Something-Or-Other, who is asked in vague and elevated language for vague and elevated abstractions. Once Auden wanted evils removed by revolutionary action, and he warned: It is later than you think . . . Later—through the last half of the 1930s, when he was all ends and no means, and saw things in the long run—he exhorted: We all know how late it is, but with Love and Understanding it is still not too late for us to . . . Last of all he prayed: Thou knowest—O save us! Some of this belongs to the bad half of what Kenneth Burke calls "secular prayer": the attempt, inside any system, to pray away, exhort away, legislate away evils that are not incidental but essential to the system.[18] Auden used to satirize the whole idea of the "change of heart." "Do not speak of a change of heart," he warned.[19] He had a deceived chorus sing vacantly: "Revolutionary worker / I get what you mean. / But what you're needing / 'S a revolution within."[20] He had come to scoff, he remained to pray: for a general moral improvement, a spiritual rebirth, Love. Remembering some of the distressing conclusions to the poems of Auden's middle period—"Life must live," Auden's wish to "lift an affirming flame"—the reader may object that this sort of thing is sentimental idealism.[21] But sentimental idealism is extraordinarily useful to someone who, after rejecting a system as evil, later accepts it—even with all the moral reservations and exhortation possible. One can pray for some vague general change of heart that will produce, automatically, all the specific changes that it would seem absurd to pray for. (Later on Auden would reject almost all of existence as evil, as "wholly other" than the God Who created it; sentimental idealism was no longer necessary, then.)

Swift believed—to quote Empson—"that everything spiritual and valuable has a gross and revolting parody, very similar to it, with the same name."[22] Similarly, everything spiritual and valuable has a sentimental and rhetorically idealistic parody; and by an unpleasant variant of Gresham's law, this parody replaces it with stupid people and discredits it with somewhat cleverer people.[23] The reactionary intellectual's instant revulsion towards anything that resembles Progress or humanitarianism is an example of the operation of this law. Auden's desire to get away from the eternal rejection of much modernist poetry managed to make the worst sections of the poems he wrote late in the 1930s no more than well-meaning gush. Such sentimental and rhetorically idealistic parodies are far more danger-ous that any gross ones could be; it is cant that barbarizes fools and confirms scoundrels. But let me quote Auden against himself (in spite of Johnson's magnificent, "Besides, besides, sir, besides,—do you not know,—are you so ignorant as not to know, that it is the highest degree of rudeness to quote a man against himself?"):[24]

And what was livelihood
Is tallness, strongness
Words and longness,
All glory and all story
Solemn and not so good.[25]

How did Auden manage to travel from a vague and aberrant com-munism to a normal enough, and temporary enough, liberalism? This was no betrayal when circumstances became unfavorable, as every now and then, once upon a time, the *New Masses* used to thun-der; long before any circumstances developed, this pilgrim was mak-ing his progress by a worn-out route.[26] During the middle 1930s there appeared in Auden a growing preoccupation with a familiar cluster of ideas: All power corrupts; absolute power tends to corrupt absolutely. Government, a necessary evil, destroys the governors. All action is evil; the will is evil, life itself is evil?[27] Our only escape lies in the avoidance of action, the abnegation of the will: to avoid action is to acquire merit, as the Lama came near to saying. Auden did not wholly or practically accept all this—who does, anywhere in the West except Los Angeles? These ideas are completely op-posed to Marxism, partially congenial to a loose extension of psy-choanalysis: as Freud has said, he was able to discover certain doc-trines only because he had not read them first in Schopenhauer.[28]

What would Freud have said about the attraction of this cluster of ideas for someone like Auden? One does not need to guess but can summarize, almost in Freud's own words: Renunciation, externally imposed, gives rise to conscience, which then demands further renunciation. Every renunciation becomes a dynamic fount of conscience; every fresh abandonment of gratification increases its severity and intolerance; every unexpressed aggression heightens the aggressiveness of the superego against the ego. The unconscious strives for complete passivity . . . No wonder Auden was attracted! This summary fits the secular Auden of the 1930s rather well, and the religious Auden of the 1940s rather better.

By means of these or similar ideas about power, action, and the will, Auden managed to make the revolutionary activity of the Early Auden seem a foolish and wicked mistake to the Liberal Auden. The true hero has become someone who, so far as anyone can see, does nothing—no one even knows he's a hero; the true saint seems, to the unknowing, one more bourgeois. One can try to reform Authority, but it would be folly to overthrow it, madness to replace it oneself: we know now that any authority is necessarily a corrupt and guilty authority—that all governors, whether they know it or not, are destroying themselves for the governed. Love is best; and Action is at best—if it ever *is* at best—a necessary evil. Everybody is guilty of everything, most of all of any willing or doing; so Auden has little heart for willing and doing, himself. He begs people to do what's best for them, he hopes and prays for them to do what's best for them; but as for his old secret-service, primitive-Christian, Little-Band-of-Consecrated-Assassins fantasies—ugh! The great symbolic action in this stage is voting, siding with the Popular Front, exposing oneself to "the flat ephemeral pamphlet and the boring meeting."[29] These are ideally suitable if one feels guilty about action; they are the least one can do. But I do not want to write more about the mechanism of Auden's change from Stage I to Stage II; these sentences are mere reminders that a fifth lecture will explain it in detail.[30]

The search for any reasons that will justify what, for other reasons, it has become necessary for us to believe—this search may have the

most protracted ramifications, but almost no one has known it to fail.
This seems rather a crude metamorphosis for so intelligent a person
as Auden? Well, as Auden says, "The windiest militant trash / Impor-
tant Persons shout / Is not so crude as our wish."[31] Who can keep
from repeating with Bolingbroke: *God knows, my son, by what bypaths
and indirect crook'd ways I met this*—position I'm in?[32] One feels sympa-
thetic toward Auden's changes and chances and choices, but mock-
ing too: they force from anyone the rueful amusement his own past
forces from him. But the painter Elstir has said all this better than
anyone is ever likely to:

> There is no man, however wise, who has not at some period of his
> youth said things, or lived in a way the consciousness of which is so
> unpleasant to him in later life that he would gladly, if he could, ex-
> punge it from his memory. And yet he ought not entirely to regret
> it, because he cannot be certain that he has indeed become a wise
> man—so far as it is possible for any of us to be wise—unless he has
> passed through all the fatuous or unwholesome incarnations by
> which that ultimate stage must be preceded. I know that there are
> young fellows, the sons and grandsons of famous men, whose mas-
> ters have instilled into them nobility of mind and moral refinement
> in their schooldays. They have, perhaps, when they look back upon
> their past lives, nothing to retract; they can, if they choose, publish
> a signed account of everything they have ever said or done; but they
> are poor creatures, feeble descendents of doctrinaires, and their wis-
> dom is negative and sterile. We are not provided with wisdom, we
> must discover it for ourselves, after a journey through the wilderness
> which no one else can take for us, an effort which no one else can
> spare us, for our wisdom is the point of view from which we come at
> last to regard the world.[33]

But let me return to Us and Them, the early Auden. We are Love;
They are hate and all the terrible perversions of love. There is an
odd, altogether ambivalent attitude toward homosexuality: in Us it is
a simple and natural relationship shading off into comradeship—like
Greek homosexuality in the historical novels of Naomi Mitchison; in

Them it is one more decadent perversion.[34] This is very plain in *The Dog Beneath the Skin*: that disreputable dive The Cosy Corner, where Jimmy "sent them crazy in his thick white socks," belongs to Them; We have the vague virtuous relationship between Alan and Francis, which the reader esteems even more than he otherwise might, since he is forced to compare it to Alan's relations with Miss Iris Crewe and Miss Lou Vipond.[35] One gets nothing approaching a Freudian analysis of this in the early Auden, Freudian as he was, though a real uneasiness about Our condition is plain in the allegorical "Letter to a Wound," implicit in the Airman's kleptomania. A contempt for women manifests itself in several imperfectly sublimated forms; "there is something peculiarly horrible about the idea of women pilots, " writes the Airman, whose (very unconvincing) love for E. has not managed to give him any prejudice in favor of her sex.[36] Sometimes this contempt is openly expressed; "All of the women and most of the men / Shall work with their hands and not think again," is the early Auden's lyrical premonition of the ideal State of the future.[37] This is not Marxism, Freudianism, or ordinary good sense. (Compare Engels's contempt at Dühring's belief that the Ideal State would have professional porters.)[38] In Auden this sort of thing was related to a Lawrence–*Golden Bough* folk-mysticism (complete with Führer, folk, blood, intuition, "the carved stone under the oak-tree") that cropped up fairly often.[39] What is wrong with it is too plain to say; but what is right about it—the insistence on a real society, the dislike of the weird isolation and individualism, the helpless rejection forced on so many of the members of our own society—ought to be mentioned. Auden has forgotten the good with the bad, and now takes the isolation of the individual—something that would have seemed impossible to almost any other society, that is the most characteristic and extravagant perversion of our own—as necessary and eternal, an absolute that can only be accepted.

We are health, They are disease; everything Auden got from Freud and Groddeck was used to put Them into the category of patients who will their own disease. Our violence is the surgeon's violence, Their opposition is the opposition of madmen to psychiatrists. We are Life, They are death. The death wish is the underlying motive for everything that They do, Auden often says or implies; if They deny it he retorts: "Naturally you're not *conscious* of it."

But I am sure that I do not need to say much more about Us and Them: the reader, whether or not he has read *The Orators*, can fill in these outlines for himself—though he could hardly arrive at some of the specific traits Auden gives the Enemy, comic peculiarities as trivial as saying *I mean* or having a room called the Den. And one will notice, without a prolonged acquaintance with the earliest poems, some of the ritual attitudes underlying them. These poems are soaked in death: as the violence of revolutionary fact, as a comprehensive symbol. Death is Their necessary and wished-for conclusion, and poems are often written from Their increasingly desperate point of view. Death belongs to Us as martyrs, as spies, as explorers, as tragic heroes—part God, part scapegoat, part criminal—who die for the people. It belongs to Us because We, Their negation, have been corrupted by Them, and must Ourselves be transcended. One is astonished to see how consistently most of the important elements of ritual (purification, rebirth, identification, and so on) are found in the early poems; their use ordinarily seems unconscious. Except for the ritual of purification by fire, all of the more common purification-rituals are plain in them. There is purification by water: in the second poem in *On this Island*, for instance, a sustained flood-metaphor shifts into parent-child imagery. There is purification through physical and spiritual decay, through the rusting-away of the machines and the diseased perversions of the men. Polar explorers are constantly being purified by icebergs and glaciers, though Auden never uses polar exploration as a strange symbol for homosexuality, as Spender does.[40] There is mountain-climbing: from these icy heights one sees differently, free of the old perspectives—one returns, like Moses, with something new. The hero's dangerous labors or journeys, his uneasy Quest, are always coming up. There is more than a suggestion of purification by sin. And the idea of rebirth is plainest of all, extending even to the common images of ontogenetic or phylogenetic development; of the foetus, new-born infant, or child; of the discontinuities of growth. The Uncle is so important partially because he is a new ancestor with whom

We can identify ourselves: Auden actually recommends "ancestor worship" of that one true Ancestor, the Uncle. By this identification with him We destroy Our real parents, Our Enemy ancestry, and thus finally abolish any remaining traces of Them in Us. Some of these elements of ritual are illustrated in the conclusion of the poem that I read last lecture, "Easter, 1929." Rebirth through death is the root metaphor here, but one also finds seasonal rebirth and the womb of the new order.

> You whom I gladly walk with, touch,
> Or wait for as one certain of good,
> We know it, we know that love
> Needs more than the admiring excitement of union,
> More than the abrupt self-confident farewell,
> The heel on the finishing blade of grass,
> The self-confidence of the falling root,
> Needs death, death of the grain, our death,
> Death of the old gang; would leave them
> In sullen valley where is made no friend,
> The old gang to be forgotten in the spring,
> The hard bitch and the riding-master,
> Stiff underground; deep in clear lake,
> The lolling bridegroom, beautiful, there.[41]

Lecture 3

When you come from the early poems to the poems of Auden's middle period, the poet's language seems to you passive and abstract. Full of adverbs and adjectives, intransitive verbs, capitalized abstractions, it is boneless by the side of that early speech, which was so packed with verbs and verbals that many of the articles, even, had been crowded out of it. The rhythms of this new language, compared to those of the old, are mechanical and orthodox or heavily perfunctory—Auden has never written so much in a sort of sloppily hypnotic accentual verse. But the rhetoric! In the middle poems, most of all in the late poems, there has grown up a system of rhetorical devices so elaborate that Auden might list it under Assets, just as a firm lists its patents. I shall name and analyze some of these devices, and illustrate them at length, since I want the reader to appreciate the weight and range of their use.

The texture of poetry depends to an extraordinary degree on the poet's sensitivity to different levels or ranges of language, to his juxtapositions, sometimes shocking and sometimes almost unnoticeable, of words from different universes or way-stations of discourse.

Everyone recognizes such extreme cases as the Elizabethans' application of a notably abstract and a notably concrete adjective, joined by *and*, to the same noun; everyone recognizes the Orators' Favorite—the insertion of an unexpectedly concrete "homely" word in an abstract context; but many of the nicer cases go unpraised and unanalyzed, though not unfelt. One of Auden's most thoroughly exploited rhetorical formulas (rhetoricians ought to distinguish it with his name) is an inversion of the Orators' Favorite: a surprisingly abstract word is put into a concrete context—in general, unexpectedly abstract, critical, "unpoetic" words, taken from relatively abstract, technical, "unpoetic" universes of discourse, are substituted for their expected and concrete sisters. The consistent use of this device is one of the things that have made people attack Auden's poetry as relaxed or essayistic or abstract; but the device, like its opposite, is merely a variety of Effect by Incongruity. Here are some examples—a few from many; most of them will be rather obvious, since the less obvious depend too much on an extensive context or an established tone to be convenient for quotation:

The beauty's set cosmopolitan smile; love's fascinating biased hand; the baroque frontiers, the surrealist police; the shining neutral summer; the tree's clandestine tide; the small uncritical islands; and the indigenous figure on horseback / On the bridle-path down by the lake; the genteel dragon; the rare ambiguous monster; the luscious lateral blossoming of woe; weep the non-attached angels; their whorled unsubtle ears; the first voluptuous rectal sins; the band / Makes its tremendous statements; the hot incurious sun; and so on.[1] In one stanza occur *the effusive welcome of the piers, the luxuriant life of the steep stone valleys,* and *beside the undiscriminating sea.*[2] Two of these last three examples are hardly examples at all: I wished to show the method degenerating into abstraction.[3]

This sort of thing is not Auden's discovery, any more than accentual verse was Hopkins's; but its bureaucratization, its systematic use as a major principle of rhetoric, is new. It is the opposite of poetic diction. There the relatively dignified and abstract is considered the only true language of poetry; here all the effect depends on the fact that the context of the poem is still concrete, so that the abstract figure is shocking against its ground.

Another of Auden's usual formulas might be called the juxtaposition of disparate coordinates: this includes the Elizabethan adjective-formula and the extension of it to three or four not-usually-coordinate terms. One finds many examples of the first (or of its familiar Shakespearean application to two nouns): *remote and hooded; nude and fabulous epochs; your unique and moping station; the noise and policies of summer; dumb and violent; deaf to prophecy or China's drum; the stoves and resignations of the frozen plains.*[4] Here are some examples of the second: *the enchanted, the world, the sad;* (spoken of the sea) *the citiless, the corroding, the sorrow; the friend, the rash, the enemy / The essayist, the able; cold, impossible, ahead; the melting friend, the aqueduct, the flower; an illness, a beard, Arabia found in a bed, / Nanny defeated, money; were they or he / The physician, bridegroom and incendiary?*[5] See how prettily a variation of the device can describe Civilization As We Know It:

Certainly our city—with the byres of poverty down to
The river's edge, the cathedral, the engines, the dogs;
Here is the cosmopolitan cooking
And the light alloys and the glass.[6]

When Auden began to use the capitalized personified abstraction, he was extremely conscious of what he was doing and meant for the reader to realize that; his use of it is intended to be unexpected and exciting, a virtuoso performance on an outmoded instrument—the reader exclaims, "Why, it works! Who'd have thought you could shoot down an airplane with a crossbow?" One finds such things as *ga-ga Falsehood; Scandal praying with her sharp kneeps up; Lust . . . muttering to his fuses in a tunnel, "Could I meet here with Love, / I would hug him to death."*[7] But showing that he could drink like a gentleman of the old school had a mesmeric attraction for Auden; in a year or two he had degenerated into an ordinary drunkard. At first he went in for all sorts of ingenious variations, and made capitalized personified abstractions out of verbs, out of adverbs, out of pronouns, out of whole phrases. But at last even his ingenuity disappeared; one saw that this trembling wretch would drink canned heat, radiator fluid, anything. In *Another Time* there is one thirteen-line menagerie in which the capitalized abstractions I Will, I

Know, I Am, I Have Not, and I Am Loved peer apathetically out from behind their bars.[8] Nearby, gobbling peanuts, throng the Brothered-One, the Not-Alone, the Just, the Happy-Go-Lucky, the Filthy, hundreds of We's and They's and Their's and Ours's and Me's, the Terrible Demon, the Lost People, the Old Masters, and the Unexpected; they feel Love and Hate and Lust and Things; above them hover all sorts of tutelary deities: the Present, the Past, the Future, the Just City, the Good Places, Fate, Pride, Charity, Success, Knowledge, Wisdom, Violence, Life and Art and Salvation and Matter and the Nightmare, Form, the State, Democracy, Authority, Duality, Business, Collective Man, the Generalized Life, the Meaning of Knowing, the Flower of the Ages, and Real Estate. Reading *Another Time* is like attending an Elks' Convention of the Capital Letters; all these last examples were taken from it, and I had not begun to exhaust the supply. There are next to none in Auden's early books.

The worst thing about such rhetorical devices, about any of the mechanisms and patented insights that make up so much of a style, is that they are habit-forming, something the style demands in ever-increasing quantities. The poet learns subtle variations or extensions he once would have thought unlikely or impossible; but he permits himself excesses, both quantitative and qualitative, that once would have appalled him. This is how styles and more than styles degenerate. Our victories are temporary victories; and nothing makes us more susceptible to a vice than the knowledge that we have already overcome it. (The fact that one once used an argument somehow seems to give one the right to ignore it.)

Everyone must have noticed all the *the's* in the poems of Auden's middle period: *the* this, *the* that, *the* other—all the thousands of categories into which beings are flung. (Contrast these poems with the early poems, in which *the's* are often omitted when required by ordinary grammar.) The bases of classification are thoroughly unsystematic, whatever comes to hand in need. The device is a convenient shorthand, short-cut, in which the type or trait is used as the unit of analysis, to obtain the building-blocks with which the passage is put together: "The glutton shall love with his mouth; to the burglar love shall mean, 'Destroy when read'; to the rich and poor the sign for 'our money'; the sick shall say of love 'It's only a phase'; the psychologist, 'That's easy'; the ****, 'Be fair.' The censor shall dream of knickers, a nasty beast. The murderer shall be wreathed with flowers; he shall die for the people."[9] This is a useful method for handling the explosive heterogeneity that everyone sees everywhere today; but the use of the method helps to explain why Auden, in his plays, gets efficient observed types, but no characters. There is plenty of journalism, fact as *summum bonum*, in Auden; his *the* method gives an illusory effect of merely pointing to the Facts, to a reality that requires neither evaluation nor explanation, but is conclusive as soon as it is shown. But Auden has far more than a good journalistic sense of the typical or immediately differentiating detail; although his differentiating characteristics are sometimes shallow or far-fetched, they are sometimes as penetrating as one could wish.

Auden depends a good deal on such devices as periphrasis: *the neat man / To their east who ordered Gorki to be electrified; the naughty life-forcer in the Norfolk jacket; that lean hard-bitten pioneer* (there follow fourteen lines: Dante); *the German who / Obscure in gas-lit London, brought* (there follow fifty lines about Marx).[10] It is easy for the rhetorical heightening this represents—the substitution of an elegant or surprising allusiveness for the proper noun—to become a vice; not so easy, though, in didactic and expository verse, where a little formal gilding comforts the yawning traveler. The same thing is true of the long, mechanically worked-out conceits that Auden begins to be fond of in the poems of his middle period, and that later become standard structural or ornamental devices. There is little use or excitement in most of them; as the new terms are mechanically generated, one stares by with lack-lustre eyes. Such conceits are particular handicaps to the lyrics: while Pascal, like Pilgrim, is finding *a passage through the caves of accusation,* and *even in the canyon of distress* gets to use *the echo of his weakness,* till at last he restores *the ruined chateau of his faith*—while this is happening a poem is being spoiled.[11]

Auden fairly early began to use words like *lovely, marvelous, wonderful, lucky, wicked* (words that are all weight and no "presentation," all attitude of subject and no description of object—that approach as a limit the "emotional noises" of the semanticists) in a peculiarly sophisticated sense. Their use is quite conscious, and implies definitely an attitude that it is hard to state definitely, but that might be paraphrased as:

"How well one knows that such words as these are looked down on by any schoolboy, as simple-silly, naive, wholly inadequate. Yet you and I know that all the most cunningly chosen figures, all the 'objective' terms, all the 'presentation' are in the end quite as inadequate—that real representation, especially of the states such words point crudely at, is impossible. You know how much better I could do; but certainly that better would still not be good enough. This time I shan't even try; the *lovely* is a license you and I tacitly condone, an indulgent and shared secret. Besides, how much of the charm and freshness and shock of the experience such a word retains; and is there not an undoubted rhetorical effectiveness about its lack either of rhetoric or of effectiveness, here in the midst of so much of both?" (Compare the way in which Churchill used to say, when some enemies of his state were prospering, that the stout heart of the English people defies these scoundrels, or anything of the kind. What such statements really mean is, "Take heart: the Present *is* the Past, the world *is* a historical romance about the combats of Black and White Knights; because we have fought, are going to fight, with the White's undoubting resolution, all shall yet be well." What chance had Hitler's speeches, straight out of the *Ring*, by the side of this literally reactionary rhetoric? For every child reads stories about knights, but few children are taken by their mothers to *Die Götterdammerung*—and in these matters it is the first step that counts.)

The tone of my paraphrase of Auden is not intended to deny the real, but precarious and occasional, effectiveness of this device of decadence. But the use of such words later degenerated into oblivious sentimentality; it had sprung from a congenital liking for such things, from a pleasure in several varieties of sentimentality that later was to borrow with relish, from James, horrors like the Great Good Place and the Real Right Thing, and to create with loving skill a brood of rival monsters.

One of the most conscious devices of the poems of the middle pe-
riod is the use of similes blunt, laconic, and prosaic enough to be star-
tling: Housman *kept tears like dirty postcards in a drawer;* in Rimbaud *the
rhetorician's lie / Burst like a pipe.*[12] One reads about *rooks / Like agile babies;*
about *Terrible Presences* that *like farmers have purpose and knowledge.*[13] Desire
like a policedog is unfastened; a phrase *goes packed with meaning like a van.*[14] As
if to show how much on order this device is, Auden once uses it three
times in five lines: poets are *encased in talent like a uniform . . . amaze us like
a thunderstorm . . . dash forward like hussars.*[15] Auden got this from Rilke,
but did not see (or could not in his practice, show that he saw) that
it is the exact rightness, the illuminating relevance, of these great
seemingly irrelevant comparisons, that make them not only effective
but give them a sort of detached classical elegance. Take Rilke's de-
scription of Eurydice being led by Hermes slowly up toward the sur-
face behind the troubled Orpheus:

> her pale hands were from the rites of marriage
> So far estranged that even the slim god's
> Endlessly gentle contact as he led her
> Repelled her as a too great intimacy.
>
> Already she was no more that fair woman
> Who often sounded in the poet's poems,
> No longer the broad conch's scented island
> Nor yonder man's possession any more.
> She was already loosened like long hair
> And given far and wide like fallen rain
> And dealt out like a stock of various goods.
> She was already rooted.
> And when, with a sudden grip,
> The god laid hold of her and as in pain
> Uttered the fatal words: He has turned round—
>
> She did not understand and murmured: Who?[16]

The long hair, the fallen rain, the stock of various goods *are* very
characteristic, but they are not just a mannerism, a sort of rhetoric;

their exact meanings are appropriate, are helping to lead up to that final *who*, which is pure imagination, pure genius, if ever a word was. The seriousness, the purity, the grave absorption in its subject of a passage like this, helps to remind us of what was most importantly lacking in Auden's work at that time. For a while Auden used these commonplace three-word similes so automatically that they had no more poetic effect than the capital letters at the start of lines: in his most Rilkean sonnets, those from *Journey to a War* and those in *The Quest*, he puts four or five in almost every poem. These short flat similes in Auden have some relation to occasional compressed and surprising metaphors; here no explanation is furnished, but one is required—of the reader: *the beast of vocation, the bars of love, the stool of madness*, and so on. And often Auden surprises by inserting slang or solecisms or colloquialisms in elevated or abstract contexts: he says of the Composer, *Only your notes are pure contraption;* and in other poems one finds *an invite with gilded edges, the identical and townee smartness, ga-ga Falsehood, the sexy airs of summer, lucky to love the new pansy railway*, and so on.[17] When he came to this country he began delightedly to exploit the treasures of American slang; how English readers must have jumped when they came on, "A bullet in Frisco put me wise / My last words were, 'God damn your eyes.' "[18] All these earlier examples are merely special cases of that insertion of a concrete word into an abstract context which is itself a special case of Effect by Incongruity, but which is too common in Auden or any poet to need illustration.

I now come to some formidable machinery which I am going to overwhelm with the even more formidable title of: The Bureaucratization of Perspective by Incongruity. Auden, who has a quick eye and an enormous range of interests, information, and insight, was at the start plunged into the very blood of the world, the Incongruous; and he found even a drop of that blood, like Fafnir's, enough to make us perceive what we could not possibly perceive without it. He began to make his poems depend more on perspective by incongruity, and less on violence, forced intensity, emotional heightening, than most other modern poetry does. But—to bureaucratize my own metaphor—so conscious and ingenious a mind was thoroughly dissatisfied with the application of a random drop or two from the blood of that disreputable old dragon the world. Why not rationalize the whole process? Why not mass together incongruities into a sort of blood bank, as ready as money, available for unlimited use in any emergency? Why not *synthesize* the Incongruous? and then (independent of natural sources, your warehouses groaning with the cheap blood poured out, in ever-increasing quantities, by that monopoly-creating secret) why not flood the world's markets, retire on the unlimited profits of the unlimited exploitation of—Incongruity?

I have been so extravagantly and mechanically incongruous because Auden has been; he has bureaucratized his method as completely, and consequently as disastrously, as any efficiency expert could wish. It is a method that can be applied to any material, a patented process guaranteed to produce insights in any quantities. The qualities, unfortunately, cannot be guaranteed. The law of diminishing returns sets in quickly; the poet's audience—one of the members of which is the poet—is as easily fatigued for incongruity as for an odor, and the poet has to supply larger and larger quantities that have less and less effect. (*The Age of Anxiety* is a wonderful illustration of what I have been saying.) The reader has seen in my earlier quotations many examples of Auden's use of this method; there exist enough examples for several generations of critics. Let me rob them of only one, a certain sort of spatial metaphor that Auden uses for people; he found it in Rilke originally.

Freud is a *climate, weather.* The *provinces* of Yeats's body *revolted; the squares of his mind were empty, / Silence invaded the suburbs, / The current of his feeling failed.*[19] Matthew Arnold is *a dark disordered city*, well equipped with *square, boulevard, slum, prison, forum, haphazard alleys, mother-farms,* and *a father's fond-chastising sky*—these in twelve packed lines.[20] One poem, "Edward Lear," ends with such a metaphor; but what it has gone through to arrive at it! Here is the poem; I italicize the unexpected or incongruous effects the poet and I want noticed:[21]

Left by his friend to breakfast alone on the white
Italian shore, his *Terrible Demon* arose

Over his shoulder; he wept to himself in the night,
A *dirty* landscape-painter who *hated his nose.*

The legions of cruel inquisitive *They*
Were *so many and big like dogs;* he was upset
By *Germans and boats;* affection was *miles away;*
But *guided by tears* he successfully *reached his Regret.*

How prodigious the welcome was. *Flowers took his hat*
And *bore him off* to *introduce him to the tongs;*
The demon's *false nose* made the *table laugh;* a *cat*
Soon had him waltzing madly, let him squeeze her hand;
Words pushed him to the piano to sing comic songs;

And children swarmed to him *like settlers. He became a land.*[22]

What critic would insult his hearers with a comment? But I should
like to mention the dangling participle I couldn't italicize (it wasn't
really the Terrible Demon who had to breakfast alone) and marvel
at how mechanical, how consciously willed, such a rhetorical pro-
cess is. Each of the biographically accurate details of the poem—
they're all *so*—is made to seem no more than another invention in
the manner of the poem; the poem, a success of a sort, is made to
seem a great deal more arbitrary than it actually is.

And now my list of illustrative quotations comes to an overpow-
ering climax, with a conceit in which Auden sees Man as two pages
of English countryside. But—two pages! I conclude weakly, with a
reference: that conceit lives on pages 298 and 299 of *The Collected Po-
etry of W. H. Auden.*[23]

All these lists of devices must by now have forced a generaliza-
tion upon my hearers: that in his later poems Auden depends to an
extraordinary degree upon rhetorical devices. I could now add to
my lists the rhetorical device of lists; but I'll leave to Auden's read-
ers the pleasure of noticing that Auden not only imitates Perse,
Joyce, Whitman, *et cetera*, but even imitates a list of Chaucer's that
Wordsworth had imitated before him. Another of Auden's practices,
not precisely a rhetorical device, has a decided effect upon the
rhetorical texture of a poem. He often writes what might be called

a *set piece*, a poem conscientiously restricted to some appropriated convention. This may even arrive at its limit, the parody; in any case, the interplay between prototype and "copy" is consistently and consciously effective—if the reader does not realize that the poem depends upon the relations to a norm of deviations from that norm, the poem will be misunderstood. It sometimes might almost be said to exist on two levels, like counterpoint—that is, like counterpoint in which one of the levels has to be supplied by the hearer. Auden, who has an acute sense of the special function and convention of a poem, and no trace of the delusion that a single poem can serve as a model for the poet's poems or for Poetry, often tries for these limited successes. When he writes a popular song, it is always a pleasure to see critics discovering that he is "influenced by popular songs"; which is like finding that Eliot's poems in French are "influenced by the French language," or like finding that Tschaikowsky's *Mozartiana* is "influenced by Mozart." Today conventions are not natural to us, and we delight in nothing so much as demanding sermons from stones, books from brooks—from every poem the more-than-what-it-gives that its convention precludes it from giving; if we are poets we may even try to furnish this. Auden has fifteen or twenty types of these set pieces: ballads, American ones especially—for instance, somewhere in that deplorable play *On the Frontier* soldiers sing an accurate parody of the ballad that begins, "I had a horse and her name was Daisy";[24] blues; Calypso songs; Gilbert and Sullivan songs; ordinary popular songs; *Don Juan* imitations; eighteenth-century witty-and-abstract-exposition-in-couplets; Anglo-Saxon riddles; doggerel nursery rhymes; hypertrophied James poetic passages, now elephantiasis-ridden as well; parodies of particular poems—"Locksley Hall," "Bryan, Bryan, Bryan," and so on.[25]

Auden's effective rhetorical use of abstraction often degenerated, in the poems he wrote during the late 1930s and the early 1940s, into the flatness and vagueness and deadness of a bad essay. *The major cause of our collapse / Was a distortion in the human plastic by luxury produced* is bad enough; later on, Rimbaud is *from lyre and weakness estranged*—one is surprised that Auden didn't finish the list with *the fair sex;* finally there is *If he succeeded, why, the Generalized Life / Would become impossible, the monolith / Of State be broken, and prevented / The cooperation of avengers.*[26] When we come to *Imperialism's face / And the international wrong* we have left verse for editorials; and *the Hitlerian monster* is like quite a number of politicians and preachers and radio announcers: it's quite like *Pravda,* for that matter.[27] Most of the poems printed for the first time in *Collected Poetry* (they are marked with a warning asterisk)[28]—most of them are written in this appallingly abstract and mechanical rhetoric, so that the reader starts out on

> That syllogistic nightmare must reject
> The disobedient phallus for the sword;
>   The lovers of themselves collect,
> And Eros is politically adored:
> New Machiavellis flying through the air
> Express a metaphysical despair,
> Murder their last voluptuous sensation,
> All passion in one passionate negation.

The reader gives an uneasy shudder, skips a couple of stanzas, and begins again:

> What pedagogic patience taught
> Preoccupied and savager elements
> To dance into a segregated charm?[29]

He realizes, then, that skipping is no good either—it's all like this; he goes back to the beginning and sets out on his dry determined path.

This degeneration into abstraction was inescapable for Auden, the reflection of his whole development. Auden's development, to a critic who knows his work well, has so much causal unity, fits together so logically and becomingly, that the critic is reluctant to break up the whole into fragments of analysis, and feels like saying with Schopenhauer: All this is a single thought. During the middle of the 1930s it was *necessary* for Auden to develop and rely upon this rhetorical machinery, since his thought and poetry were becoming increasingly abstract, public, and prosaic. These rhetorical devices constitute a quasi-scientific method by which one can make rhetorically effective any material, by which even the dead or what has never lived can be galvanized into a forbidding animation. (It is easy to imagine the later Auden's paying quite a sum for some rhetorical device which has escaped his reading, and would be useful in his writing; but it is not at all easy to think of the device.) The earliest poems do not need and do not have such a rhetoric.

Auden wished to make his poetry more logical, better organized, more orthodox, more easily understood; he finally became one of the clearest poets who ever lived; with these good intentions, he managed to run through a tremendous series of changes so fast that all of his poetry was hurt and some of it—the lyrics especially—ruined. In Auden's later poems one finds everything that money can buy: i.e., everything that the most extensive information, the most laborious ingenuity, and the most professional production know-how (hindered, adulterated, or occasionally transfigured by that obstinate survivor, genius) can manage to produce. The poems are the work of a real Man of Letters. (It is these Letters that kill.) Many of the early poems give the reader the impression that they have been produced by Auden's whole being, are as much unconscious as conscious, have necessarily been made just as they are; often they must have surprised Auden almost as much as they surprise us. The best of them have shapes, as driftwood and pebbles do, that seem the direct representation of the forces that produced them. Most of the later poems represent just as directly the forces that produced *them*: the head, the head, the top of the head; the abstract, reasoning, fanciful, idealistic, sentimental Intellect. Nietzsche wrote, "Euripides as a poet is essentially an echo of his own conscious knowledge."[30] This terrible sentence fits much of the later Auden as if it had been made for him. (All his long, witty, expository, didactic poems began in light verse—in the long *Don Juan* imitation in *Letters from Iceland*—and they have never wholly escaped their origin.) Much of this later poetry gets its general conformation from a particular necessity: the necessity of writing a great deal of poetry, year after year, without emotional and imaginative exhaustion. Any half-dozen of Auden's best

early lyrics represent far more *strain*—of compression, of organiza-
tion, of "realization," of emotional imagination under imposed con-
ditions, of the poet's feeling himself into the things of this world—
than the longest poem like *New Year Letter* or *The Age of Anxiety*.

How conscious and rational and controlled is poetry? can poetry
afford to be? There has been no age too rationalistic or neoclassical
to feel that somehow, say what one will, genius *is* its own law; that
there is in poetry something deep, obscure, and powerful that can
neither be explained nor disregarded; that art is not merely a "craft,"
is not really—as Collingwood has shown so well—a craft at all.[31]
Auden's later method is willed, produced at will, willful; it is the
magic of Blackstone and Houdini, not the Magic of the douanier
Rousseau and the *Märchen*. All excellent things are difficult, men
used to say; these poems are too easy for us, too easy for Auden.
The later poetry is, by any standards, an astonishingly Alexandrian
affair. Wherever we look, from the *Iliad* to "During Wind and Rain,"
we can see that the rational intelligence guides and selects, that it
does not produce and impose; we make our poetry, but we make it
what we can, not what we wish. Everyone knows, after Freud and
the case histories, what happens to us when we impose on ourselves
unacceptable and unbearable restrictions. Poetry—which repre-
sents the unconscious as well as the conscious, our lives as well as
our thoughts; and which has its true source in the first and not the
second—is as easily and fatally perverted. The sources of poetry are
delicate and unaccountable, and open and close for no reason that
the poet or anyone else can see—are dried up by too-rigorous su-
pervision; the springs of verse are always full.

I should like to discuss in this lecture, out of its proper chrono-
logical sequence, the work in which Auden's rhetoric comes to its
last terrible fruition.[32] That, surely, is *The Age of Anxiety*: it is a work
that is almost impossible for a lover of Auden's poetry to be just to;
while one reads it, one feels that the man who, during the 1930s,
was one of the five or six best poets in the world, has gradually
turned into a rhetoric-mill grinding away at the bottom of Limbo,
into an automaton that keeps making brilliant little jokes, extraor-
dinary little plays on words, unbelievable little rhetorical engines, as

compulsively and unendingly and uneasily as a neurotic washes his hands. A poet has turned into a sack of reflexes: Auden no longer has to struggle against standard tricks, set idiosyncrasies, behavior-adjustments aged into obsessive behavior—it is these, put into autonomous operation, that write the poem; you almost feel that Auden could be psychoanalyzed by laying on a couch and reading *The Age of Anxiety* to the analyst.

Much of *The Age of Anxiety* is supposed to be thought or said by four different characters, but they are seldom more than four chairs, believed in as chairs, in which Auden takes turns sitting. Male and female, Gentile and Jew, are one in the sight of Auden; the method of the serious passages, at bottom, is exactly that of the comic passages, *The Age of Anxiety* is "about" the Seven Ages of Man, landscapes, war, God, everything, anything; after all, if you treat everything alike, any subject is as good as any other, and you might as well give yourself room for completely free association. If a boat is torpedoed and the men die, you pity them but still . . . What is it, after all? One more opportunity, one more demand, for one more piece of rhetoric; you make your regular plays on words, write

They swallowed and sank, ceased thereafter
To appear in public; exposed to snap
Judgments of sharks, to vague inquiries
Of ameboid monsters, mobbed by slight
Unfriendly fry.[33]

Is something else required of poets?[34]

Page after page the poem keeps saying: *The real subject of poetry is words.* (Words have seldom been better used, and seldom worse: it is the whole, not just the parts, that is a mistake.) One understands what Auden meant when he said, in a recent review, that all art is so essentially frivolous that he prefers it to embody beliefs he thinks false, since its frivolity would degrade those he thinks true. This sounds like an indictment of art, but it is also a confession of Auden's, and *The Age of Anxiety* is the evidence that substantiates the confession. It is the sort of poem that an almost absolutely witty and almost absolutely despairing dictionary would write. In one sense it is a remarkably honest, revealing, self-exposing poem. Underneath the jokes and fantasies and sermons there is a chaotic, exhausted confusion; all the moral sentiments are solemn, hollow whistles in the dark, all the frivolity is the frivolity of a world in which everything is dying away into a senseless dream, "self in self steeped and pashed—quite / Disremembering, dismembering all now."[35] (During the late 1940s Auden's poetry, which had been under extraordinary moral, political, and theological tension for many years, now and then collapsed into the most abject frivolity, and one would encounter in some random poem or review an Apollo who blurted out, in a strange new tone of acquiescence and exhaustion, that man's real duty is to go out and get drunk with the boys: surely there have never been sentences more uneasily and helplessly and heartbreakingly Dionysian.)

When I reviewed *The Age of Anxiety* very unfavorably a few years ago, I felt more or less in the position of that lovely little boy who watched the emperor's new clothes go shivering by, so that I finished by saying, "But believe me if you can: that morning coat, that rich and modest necktie, that simple but assertive pin, are nothing but delusions of the reviewers, occupational phantasmagoria of people who are reviewing not one bad poem by Auden, but Auden." Later I met so many people who felt it was bad, and read so many English reviews condemning it (it was published much later in England), that I felt I could have spoken with quiet confidence instead of yelling to convince the unwilling.[36] For what it is, *The Age of Anxiety* is sometimes well and sometimes brilliantly done; it is what it is that is so troubling to the reader. It is a strange Alexandrian document; archaeologists, hundred of years later will be able to read it and say, "yes, this is what they were anxious about then." As for what they *weren't* anxious about then, that isn't treated—the world of the poem is a world in which everything has gone complicatedly wrong; and Auden is exactly the poet to think of so many complicated and varied and exact details of the wrongness that the innocent reader will helplessly agree, "Yes, he's mentioned everything—this *is* the world." There is a book called *The Armed Vision* which gives a most impressive picture of what the ideal critic would know: it can be summed up briefly, in the word *everything*.[37] *The Age of Anxiety* is almost the sort of poem such a critic would write. No poet I can remember has ever been able to think of the world in the terms in which dozens of different sorts of technicians think of it, as easily as Auden. Yet this does seem an odd thing for a poet to be willing to do—isn't it beneath him, really? . . . and in twenty or thirty years when most of those technical terms, ways of thinking, are old-fashioned or forgotten, what *will* the poem read like then?

Some of the rhetoric in *The Age of Anxiety* is an extravagantly accomplished and professional job, done as nothing but genius could do it. There is a whole new generation of the most ingenious and disingenuous devices that any poet has ever used—except Joyce, whose *Finnegans Wake* has considerably influenced Auden in this poem; there are surrealist devices that Hieronymus Bosch would envy; rhetorical devices as extraordinary as the new class of large-dictionary words that ornament them: *virid* and *pinguid*, *desial*, and *fucoid* and *louch*. I can't pronounce these, but who can? Who can even tell whether he is mispronouncing them? There are gleams of Auden, the real Auden, here and there among these skillfully, comprehensive, somehow irrelevant pages: one reads and hopes; but then one comes upon some dreary facetiousness that would embarrass a comedian on the radio:

> Listen courteously to us
> Four reformers who have founded—why not? –
> The Gung-Ho Group, the Ganymede Club
> For homesick young angels, the Artic League
> Of Tropical Fish, the Tomboy Fund
> For blushing Brides and the Bride-a-wees
> Of Sans-Souci, assembled again
> For a Think-Fest.[38]

Why not?—It is the motto of the poem. The poem itself—as Auden might mockingly admit: I don't know—is the best example of the disease that it diagnoses.[39]

Lecture 4

When one thinks about the faults of Auden's early poems, they are usually not faults that we *hold against* the poet or the poem—let me call them *Isn't it a pity that* faults. They are faults of organization, of focus: the poem seems good, but not as autonomous, as concentrated and unified, as largely and heavily *there* in the midst of its world, as we could wish; so that we feel, Isn't it a pity that so much originality and individuality and rightness of texture weren't concentrated into a few intense, imposing, completely realized concretions? The poems are, many of them, thoroughly successful for what they are, and they feel to us, as a whole body of poetry, live and right and memorable, something to be read over and over, year after year; but the best poems do not stand out from the others, as big dazzling successes, in the way in which a poet's best poems usually do—after reading a couple of them to people one always feels like hurrying on and reading others, *lots* more, in order to give the reader a truthful impression of Auden's early work. And even that isn't enough: one wants to read them over and over and over, to make sure that he really knows them, gets them.

The faults that one finds in Auden's middle and later poems are of a different kind, ones that we do hold against the poems and the poet. Auden had become a much more professional poet, in one sense: he had become particularly good at making a poem *this particular poem*, at making its unity and organization plain to anybody; he had, at command, a notably large assortment of techniques, of rhetorical devices, and he had, to a degree perhaps unprecedented among modern poets, a sense of his audience, a direct relationship to it—many of his poems were almost speeches to Auden's Audience, letter to Auden's Audience, *as it then was*; when, by the middle of the forties, that Audience had changed out of all recognition, it found that those poems had changed out of all recognition too, and exclaimed in horror, "You mean that that little man with the curls and club foot was *our Byron*?" Being the Byron of our days—that is, *the* symbolic figure a whole generation of readers looks up to, finds itself embodied in—is a primitive, dramatic, daemonic thing; Auden took to it very naturally (he had always been just this to his disciples and readers at Oxford), took to it so naturally that his poetry was transfigured in the process of adapting itself to his new wider role, his new larger audience. What is wrong with the poems he wrote from *The Dance of Death* on through the 1930s, up into the 1940s, almost always, in one form or another—sometimes a very sublimated form—is a too-early success, a slightly vulgar or crude or too-direct appeal, a sure-fireness, some variant of which Virgil Thomson calls the "wow technique."[1] Auden became a master at *moving an audience as he wished it to be moved*, became a true and magical rhetorician. When you read a poem like "Spain 1937"– which was even printed separately as a pamphlet—you realize that you are reading the work of the *real* Poet Laureate of that generation—a particular segment of it, of course— a man who could speak to and for that whole audience *as it conceived itself*, about the "real" problems, the "real" realities, of its world—*as it conceived them*. Later on the audience found that it had not been what it thought itself, nor had its world been what it thought it; *then*, when it reread "Spain 1937," it was as embarrassed by the poem as by any of those World War I Liberty Loan speeches that Auden had always enjoyed parodying. I will read it, point out some of the things that

seem to me particularly interesting about it, and then we might dis-
cuss anything else the audience finds characteristic or strange:[2]

[Reads "Spain 1937."]

Notice the more than Tschaikowskyish, the extraordinarily *obvi-
ous* structure of the poem, the *yesterday, today, tomorrow* triad, a sort
of hourglass corset for the poem. The audience's perception of the
structure is part of its pleasure in the poem, and we almost expect it
to chorus each *yesterday* or *today* or *tomorrow* as a Negro congregation
choruses *Amen*. Notice how, by doing one of the things he's fondest
of doing, using all the concrete, learnèd, and sometimes surprising
details of the past—no poet of this century has used information,
knowledge, intelligence, as effectively and exhaustively as Auden—
Auden not only gets some poetic life and immediacy into the ab-
straction Yesterday, the abstraction History, but manages to make
the hearers of the poem feel that that the poem knows all about the
past; the advertisements of antiseptics always say, *Science says*, and
this poem says—so to speak—*History says*. (Notice how the accen-
tual verse puts a sort of impressive half-hypnotic oratorical empha-
sis upon the principal words, makes you read everything heavily in
order to make it plain that it *is* verse; the relationships of the verse
to the subject-matter seems cruder and more direct that it does in
good accentual-syllabic verse; compare the metre of this poem with
the metre of say "Pleasure Island" in Auden's new book.[3] But when
the poet has established this History he *doesn't* show the future as its
inevitable result, *doesn't* comfort us with the inevitable withering
away of the state; when the rational, the individual lives, appeal to
that History, even in its most generalized form as Evolution, to do
once more what it has always done, it replies that it no longer *does*
anything, "Not today, not to you"; it is only what *you* do, your con-
scious choice; Necessity is—we learn to our complete dismay, our
conscience-stricken horror—Necessity is only our aggregate Free
Will. Then Auden cheers us up by showing us how well many have
answered this "challenge," in the "*corrupt* heart of the city," in the
"long expresses that lurch through the *unjust* lands"; *they*, the pure
and just opposites, came to Spain "*to present their lives.*" Because of
them "tomorrow, *perhaps*, the future."

The poem has the shape of an hour glass with tomorrow and yesterday at each broad end, today in the narrow middle:[4] the romantic and complicated variety of the past leads to the romantic and complicated variety of the future, through a sort of absolutely simple Thermopylae, a moral razor's edge, where only one choice, moral act, can pass at a time: Today *is* the moment of choice, our deciding to enlist, to *do* something, and it is only by means of this absolute black and white simplicity that the future can come into existence at all. But if the Today of the poem is crude, the *your vote or your life* of the popular orator, what shall we say of the Future? *The research on fatigue / And the movement of packers?* The *enlargement of consciousness by diet and breathing* (hasn't he got mixed up? this is *Tomorrow?* Isn't this *Yesterday?* Or isn't this Isherwood, not Auden)? *The rediscovery of romantic love?* (This is like rediscovering the locomotive; and it's a particularly odd thing for Auden to say, considering how many romantic love-poems he'd written and was to write.) *The photographing of ravens* (it's just as if that movie about English bird-watchers, the one called *The Tawny Pipit*, were introduced to us as *The Shape of Things to Come*)? *All the fun under / Liberty's masterful shadow* (Here words fail me—few men, few women, and few children have ever written anything as silly, as shamefully silly, as *amazingly* silly as this)—under the masterful shadow of *this* line things like *the hour of the pageant-master* and *the poets exploding like bombs* look like nothing but ordinary tripe; and yet really the *poets exploding like bombs* is worthy of the Stalin Prize. Then we're given some details of *today*: notice how extraordinarily abstract and statistical they are to begin with, how extraordinarily unreal and *Journey's End*ish they are in the second stanza.[5] *The inevitable increase in the chances of death* sounds like an insurance company's remark on a change in the climate, not a *bit* like "You've got a good chance of getting killed if you enlist with the Loyalists"; *the conscious acceptance of guilt in the fact of murder* sounds like a wonderfully tame and priggish *Address to the Pacifists of Oxford; the expending of powers / On the flat ephemeral pamphlet and the loving meeting* is remarkably funny as a sort of makeshift consolation addressed to intellectuals and Creative people—they *are* wasting their powers on the flat ephemeral thing, Life, but it's necessary Today, and Tomorrow, thank goodness, everything will be all right again. Then the next stage is pure *Journey's End*, though what people called the "latent homosexuality" of that play seems rather more overt here.⁶ The last stanza is a triumph of rhetoric, of making the audience do what *you* want by giving them what *they* want. *The stars are dead* get over well both the audience's conviction that religion and the Moral Order, man's magical helpers, are a construction of the past that can't help us *now*, and the audience's feeling that Today is *different*, that our problems are *really* different, qualitatively different, from those of the past; and the line divorces man from Nature, too. *The animals will not look* probably occurred to Auden because of Rilke's line, but it divorces us from the old simple evolutionary process, says that there's no regression possible for us, that we human beings are alone in this world except for other human beings, must save ourselves.⁷ *We are left alone with our day* (how different from James's *He was left alone with the quiet day*)⁸ brings over all the fatal shortness and immediacy and precarious human daylight of this view of things; *the time is short* is not half so hastening, shortening, as the *and* before it and the *and* after it, at the end of the line; and History (back in business now as a fatal and judging, but helpless, Power) may be able to pity us if we fail, but it won't be able to help us—nor will it be able to *pardon* us, to *forgive* us: it's up to us, right now, completely up to us, and if we fail it our *fault*, and everything's done for.

Would it be unjust to say that the powers of the poet are willingly and successfully prostituted, in this poem, to the demands of a particular time, a particular audience, a particular task? This is symbolic of what Auden did to a lesser extent in a great many of his poems. In this poem how well Auden knows what he is! how well he knows exactly what he is doing! Yet as we read the poem, and think of it and of the poet and his readers, all of this can't help seeming to us a comedy arranged by a pageant-master with an unusually grim and mocking taste in pageants. How well-meaning and fooled and moral and rhetorical they all were! "Whom God misleads is well misled," as Goethe said, and the Spirit of the Age is an efficient substitute for God. How much better off Auden *would* have been if he'd said he-knew-not-quite-what to an audience that couldn't quite make out what he meant. Rilke said that for the first twelve or fifteen years he read poetry to audiences he had only one poem that was sure of making an effect, and that was because of its subject: a carousel.[9] Auden had many dozens of poems—some of them pretty good poems, too—that he could be sure would always have their effect on those audiences. The poems are what they were; but where can you find one of those audiences? In the long run it pays to write for the ages, because the ages are the only things that are left.

But these faults are the faults of one of the best of living poets; after having talked so much about [them], I should like to talk for a while, quite generally, about Auden's virtues.[10] I have already spoken at great length about the virtues of Auden's early work: some of these later disappear, though some of them are replaced by new ones. But there are a great many noticeable virtues that one sees in Auden's work as a whole:

He is not only extremely intelligent but also—and this is a much rarer thing—extremely intelligent *in* his poetry; he manages to put an astonishing amount of intelligence, acute insight, into effective use in his poems. Ideas, theories, dialectic are material for him as they have been material for few other poets; he uses abstractions, sets of ideas, astonishingly naturally and well—too well and too naturally, sometimes, for they keep him from writing about other more recalcitrant things.

He has an extraordinary wideness of range, of subject-matter, of information: pointing to the world, he could say with some truth: "Why, I can write about any of it—*have* written about most of it." No other living poet gives so much the feeling of having the whole range of things, facts, and ideas and events, the actual objective world, more or less at their disposal. In the phrase *more or less*, the word *less* stands for the less pleasant fact that a great deal of all this the poet can only refer to, treat with a brilliant superficial phrase, make part of a brilliant superficial image. (But it is *most* ungrateful to look such a gift in the mouth: after all, most poets couldn't use most of these things in any way if they knew they exist[ed].) Auden really has seen men and their cities, read their books, looked at their pictures, heard their music, thought their thoughts—and almost everything he has done or heard about is at his command, astonishingly so. A slower and profounder thinker, a man with more empathy for more people, an uneasier and humbler spirit, would not be able to use so much so freely.

He is an extraordinarily witty, or funny writer: he has at his fingertips most of the incongruities of existence: the ranges and levels of his wit and humor are astonishing.

He is a great technician, is as *professional* a poet as anybody alive. He has an astonishingly varied and objective skill with metre, rhyme, organization, and is wonderfully good at particularizing a poem, at making it just this poem. He is thoroughly old-fashioned in his ability to write to order, in his ability to do exactly what this particular work calls for *just here*. If the work demands at this point a comic sestina in the style of Henry James, using as its six rhyme-words the names of six of the seven sleepers of Ephesus, Auden's eyes gleam, light up, sparkle, and he has it done by tea-time.[11] (My hearers may feel: "But what work ever demanded such a sestina as this?" Well, Auden's works often do.) Of all modern poets of any merit, Auden is the most facile and the most fertile, has the quickest and most sparkling mind.

He is, perhaps, the greatest living rhetorician; has a more extraordinary command of language than almost anyone else alive. What other poet can do so *many* different things with words? Because he has depended so much on rhetoric—has depended too much on rhetoric—his rhetorical powers have undergone an extraordinary elaboration and specialization; he has done time and time again what nobody else could do, could think of doing, or could want to do.

He is an extremely novel and original poet, but at the same time has extraordinary gifts of imitation, of mimicry, of taking and making his own. He is unusually skillful at analyzing someone else's work, taking out what he likes, and synthesizing a new style of his own that will include this. (As the reader will have noticed, all these qualities I have been talking about show that Auden is, in most of his work, an unusually objective and conscious writer; few poets have liked to work, been able to work, so much in the glare of daylight, from the clear accessible surface of the mind.[)]

He has a really unusual ability to make a poem not only a unit, a particular little world, but an immediately different, immediately engrossing one. The first and last thing you feel about Auden is that he has an angelic or diabolical gift just for *being interesting*. He sees everything, when he tries, in an effectively different or unusual way: by *effectively* I mean that he sees things just differently enough to astonish and delight his readers, rarely differently enough to really puzzle them, to make them take years to get used to his new way of seeing things—his poems, except for the early ones, are not poems which have—as Wordsworth said about his own poems, as Proust said about Beethoven's later quartets—to create their own audience.[12] I remember, from freshman chemistry, that some solutions were full of things called *free ions*—or perhaps *radicals*—which went roaming through [them] seeking whatever they could join themselves to.[13] It seems to me that Auden is just such a free, roaming, unattached, unscrupulous intelligence, able to join itself to almost anything and to make poetry—good, bad, or indifferent, but poetry—out of it. Such an ion is most a comedian just when it is most solemn, most joining-itself-to-the-Universe. The funniest section of the *Chartreuse de Parme* is the section in which Fabrizio becomes the most popular preacher in Parma—I can never read some of Auden's sermons without being reminded of Fabrizio's, and smiling delightedly at the bright, restless, surreptitious, insatiable eyes darting at the congregation from out of the serious uplifted face.[14] All this goes with Auden's singular gift—he had it even in his first years at Oxford, apparently—for making his poems seem (as of course they are) manifestations of an important and unique being, an Extraordinary Personality—he is better at this than anybody since Yeats and Eliot. He has been, for a very long time now, a Public Figure, a Leader, a man with a Rôle; he sometimes seems to be living in that Crystal Palace in which Victorian politicians or Great Men lived, permanently on exhibition, and you think of Auden as an odd compound of Disraeli, Tennyson, and Sydney Smith.[15]

Auden has a wide though relatively shallow knowledge of people, and an insatiable curiosity about all their manifestations; this is one of the things that helps to make his poetry as interesting as it is. He

is a genuinely humane, humanistic writer, someone whose first inter-
est is in people, their actions, ideas, emotions: at the seashore he
stares at the people at the bathing beach and despises the sea.[16] He
is a spider with lines out to people, not a tree with roots in people;
and he knows about them—has information about them—more than
he really feels about them, most of the time.[17] Very typically, he has
one of the shepherds say at Bethlehem: "The solitude familiar to the
poor / Is feeling that the family next door, / The way it talks, eats,
dresses, loves, and hates, / Is indistinguishable from one's own."[18] It's
easy to know this about the poor if you don't know any poor people
except in graphs, tables, or books; and can ignore the ways they feel
about themselves; I don't know too much about the poor, but I *have*
lived with them for years in barracks, and they're *not* indistinguish-
able, not solitary, and they don't feel that they are either.[19] Auden
knows comparatively little about families, about ordinary private
lives, anyway; he has had an extraordinarily public life himself, and
when he talks about these ordinary private lives ordinary human be-
ings have, he is almost always talking down, nature-faking, telling
you how Mama Grizzly feels about little Wob, her backward cub.

One of Auden's most obvious virtues is this: he has almost com-
pletely escaped from the limitation, the specialization, of "mod-
ernist" poetry. (At the same time he has lost some of the "modernist"
virtues that his early work still had.) You can say the same thing, so
far as Auden is concerned, about many of the more obvious limita-
tions or specializations of romantic poetry. I suppose that he would
be, of all modern poets, the easiest for Pope or Byron to become ac-
customed to.

Another of Auden's virtues is his great capacity for growth or
change—he is as incapable as a chameleon of keeping the same sur-
face for any great length of time. It is rather queer and pathetic to
mention as a virtue this capacity for change, in the case of a man
who changed away from his best poetry, got steadily worse, for
many years; but he *has* begun to get better again, and is *not* laid
away in that real graveyard of poets, My Own Style, going on like
a repeating decimal until the day someone drives a stake through
his heart.

Auden's willingness to be emotional or sentimental is a great virtue, a real necessity, in the case of so brilliant and restless an intelligence; although it often produces absurdly and revoltingly sentimental poems, it also allows real sentiment, genuine emotion, and protects Auden from the hardness, the rejecting self-protective superiority, of some modern poets. His latest poetry is often the poetry of a man full of dry tired knowledge, in whom a little weak emotion convalesces among reviews; the lack of obvious emotion, of sentimentality, is impressive because it seems natural, *not* an effective role or stylistic device.

One of the most noticeable virtues of Auden's poems is their great variety—I cannot think of any poet, ever, who has written more different *sorts* of poems. There is a protean complication to his work; and since the world has this complication, too, Auden's poetry is unusually suited for mirroring or representing it. There used to be a famous joke about physicists: that in explaining the behavior of the atom they used quantum mechanics on Monday, Wednesday, and Friday, and ordinary classical physics on Tuesday, Thursday, and Saturday. This joke always made me wonder: What do they do on Sunday? Go to church and say that there's no contradiction between religion and science? sleep late and read the funnies? die of unrequited love? Auden resembles these physicists, though *he* doesn't have one method for odd days, one for even, *he* has a separate method for every hour of Monday, Tuesday, Wednesday, Thursday, Friday, and Saturday. But I always wonder about him, as I do about the physicists: What *does* Auden do on Sunday? What *does* Auden think about the world just for private consumption, when he doesn't have to put what he thinks in *any* form, say what he thinks to *any* reader? This is rather like asking: What is Churchill like as a private figure, in private life? The answer to *that* question is, surely: Churchill isn't like *anything* as a private figure; the question is meaningless. You might as well ask, "What is Churchill like as a nursing mother?" Our answer to a suitable question about Auden will be a very different one, yet it *will* resemble this answer a good deal more than it would if we were answering such a question about you or me or the man next door. It is hard not to feel (if we judge by those po-

ems of Auden's which ostensibly express his deepest and most per-
sonal feelings) that public life has invaded his private life to an un-
usual degree; so that when we read all the poems that, in *Nones*,
seem to come from vacation or retirement, it is from the vacation or
retirement of an important public figure: their disenchantment is
the experienced, professional disenchantment of someone accus-
tomed to power and the Great World.

But let me, after this considerable digression into Auden's quali-
ties, return to his virtues. If at times he moralizes too much, he is at
the same time a genuinely moral poet, a complicated, caring, wor-
rying human being who remembers that life is a demanding
predicament; who knows that guilt and grief and remorse, all our at-
tempts at goodness, are awful to us, but awfully attractive too—are,
for all of us, inescapable.[20] There is no real reason for stopping here
in my catalogue of Auden's virtues, since he has many others that
my hearers could remind me of, and that I could remind my hearers
of; but I want to stop considering them in this abstract form, and get
back to them in the concrete and relatively novel form in which we
find them in Auden's last book, which is, I think, the best book that
he has published in a number of years.[21]

Auden's new book is named *Nones*. *Nones* means—as you may al-
ways have known, but as I knew only through having looked it up
in the dictionary—"the daily office of the church originally said at
the ninth hour, three in the afternoon"; it is also the old spelling of
nonce. Auden has always liked giving temporal titles to his work—
Another Time, "For the Time Being"—and this one is so good, so ex-
actly applicable, that it disarms criticism, and invites Appreciation.
It is the hour at which Christ was put up on the cross, the hour of
flat reality. In the *real* dark night of the soul, Auden feels, it is always
three o'clock in the afternoon: you can see everything that is there,
which is what was there, which is what will be there—there is noth-
ing else to see, and you do not see it; it is the perfect hour to de-
spair, or to play solitaire, or just to take a nap. It is the hour of a dis-
enchantment which takes itself for granted, of an anticlimax which
has forgotten, or smiles indifferently at, its own old climaxes: as Au-
den says, in the title poem of the book, "the wind has dropped and

we have lost our public."[22] [Auden's public is still there, of course, but Auden has become surprisingly indifferent to it and allows it to become rather indifferent to him; the most professional of magicians is the one who gets bored with magic, who at last *really* has nothing up his sleeve, not even his arm; and the most professional of orators is the one who finally gets tired of fooling and moving his audiences and who, then, *pleases himself*, talking dryly, elaborately, and conversationally, using art to conceal art, and inverting or reversing half his old devices.] At this third hour of the afternoon, as Auden says in the same poem, we can't "remember why / [we] shouted or what about / So loudly in the sunlight this morning . . . we are left alone with our feat."[23] How wonderfully different from the *We are left alone with our day* that helps conclude "Spain 1937."[24] That word *feat* is peculiarly deadly, peculiarly calm, like the "dead calm" of this hour. Auden uses his consciousness of how different everything has come to seem to him now, of how different he has permitted himself to become, to write one of the three or four best poems of the book, a surprisingly original poem about—but the poem is careful never to mention the subject; that is part of its originality. (Our feat, we find out later, was the crucifixion.) Breughel painted a crucifixion in which, after a good deal of searching, you can barely make out Christ, there in the midst of the surging, Flemish-oriental holidaying crowd; but this is a crucifixion with no Christ, no cross, no Jerusalem—a football game with nobody left in the stands but the janitors picking up the Coca-Cola bottles and the peanut shells. Let me read you the poem:[25]

[Reads "Nones."]

It is a good poem, an original poem, a strange poem to be written by everyone's *enfant terrible*, by someone who was saying only a few years ago, that he supposed "my friends will say until I turn my toes up . . . why *doesn't* Wystan ever grow up?"[26] There is, in this poem, not a milligram of boyish charm. The fact is, Auden *has* grown up, he's not only grown up, he's grown old—as old as Talleyrand. So many of these poems are poems written by someone who is past, has gotten over, almost everything. He often reminds one of Talleyrand or Disraeli or Stendhal at Civitavecchia or such—and I notice that "the tired old diplomat" has become a regular fig-

ure in his poems.[27] He has got so convincingly old, or so irrevoca-
bly, unexcusably middle-aged (and, in a sense, the really middle-
aged are older than the old), that once or twice he sounds almost
like Frost—for instance, when he says about animals:

> Let them leave language to their lonely betters
> Who count some days and long for certain letters;
> We, too, make noises when we laugh or weep,
> Words are for those with promises to keep.[28]

The change in the poems prepares you for the change in Auden
himself, who is no longer a lank towheaded slouching boy, but
looks at you with a lined, sagging, fretful, consciously powerful old
lion's face.

Auden said in 1940, "For I relapse into my crimes, / Time and
again have slubbered through / With slip and slapdash what I do, /
Adopted what I would disown, / The preacher's loose immodest
tone."[29] He said this, and it was so; and for how many years after-
wards it kept on being so: if during the 1930s he had preached, with
slip and slapdash, the Popular Front, during the first half of the
1940s he preached, with as much slip and as much slapdash, as
much rhetoric and sentimentality and attitudinizing, as much talent,
his own idiosyncratic version of Barth and Niebuhr and
Kierkegaard. He disapproved of what he was doing, perhaps, but
how he liked doing it! And yet one day he stopped liking it; he was
tired. How much of his sentimentality, and stained-glass attitudes,
and Moving Rhetoric, he also began to be tired of! In fact, disin-
genuous creature that he is, he began sometimes to pretend that
there was nothing there to *be* tired of; he began to pretend that he
had always been on the other side, the side of the Resistance, in the
great war between Morality and Fun, the great war between Doing
as We Ought and Doing as We Please. He began to specialize—be-
tween regressions into moralizing—in scornful and amusing and
charmingly and precisely funny denunciations of "pompous Apollo"
and all his works; *Auden* was—had always been—surprise, sur-
prise!—on the side of Hermes, god of thieves and business men.

Strike out those *thieves and business men*, whom Auden is careful never to mention; *this* is a Hermes whose sons, I quote, "love to play."[30]

One of Housman's poems tells how, long ago, "couched upon her brother's grave / The Saxon got me on the slave"—and how now, on the "marches of my breast," the "truceless armies yet / Trample, rolled in blood and sweat; / They kill and kill and never die / And I think that each is I."[31] Surely Auden too is writing about a war which had gone on for a long time in the marches of *his* breast; how often the Inside, the Unconscious, the Original Auden, must have smiled mockingly, demonically, at what the Conscious Outside was telling everybody to do—smiled, and gone about its living. In some of these last poems the Conscious and Moral Auden is, quite consciously and immorally, coming to terms with the Unconscious Auden by going along with it, by letting it have its way—and not just in life, where we can and do gloss over anything—but in poems, which are held against us by us and everyone else.

Auden has, perhaps, always made such impossible moral demands on himself and everybody else partly because it kept him from having to worry about satisfying more ordinary, moderate, possible demands; he had, perhaps, preached so loudly, made such extraordinarily sweeping gestures, in order in the commotion to hide himself even from himself. But he seems, finally, to have got tired of the whole affair, to have become willing to look at himself *without doing anything about it*, without even shutting his eyes or turning his head away, or denouncing everyone else for being no better: in some of these latest poems he seems to accept himself for whatever he is, the world for whatever it is, without even wanting to immediately convert both into rhetoric and sentimentality and effective attitudes as he does so often in his bad poems. In his last book he lies back in himself as if he were an unmade bed, and every cell in his sleeping complacent face seems to be saying: "But when did anybody ever get up? Whoever's fool enough to make a bed?" Take the first poem in *Nones*; many of you will be familiar with it as one of the poems he reads on the Columbia record called *A Pleasure-Dome of Poetry*.[32] This poem, "Prime," seems to me one accurate just as observed, relevant, inescapable fact—real fact, not the more effective journalistic, local-color, in-the-know substitute that often tempted Auden almost as strongly as it did Kipling. A poem like "Prime" is never going to take the place of "To a Nightingale"—on the other hand, it doesn't claim that it will; it is a surprising quiet, accurate, unassuming poem: the heroics at the end (imagine what Auden would have made of them eight or ten years ago!) are so muted that they hardly seem heroics at all, but an uncomfortable truth. And we notice (what a good many other poems in the book, some better, some worse, also make us notice) that Auden has become, probably, the most *professional* poet in the world; there is an extraordinary sureness, a calm taking-itself-for-granted skill, behind the easy matter-of-factness of some of these poems—more skill than there was in some of the showiest, splashiest, most technically spectacular poems of the late 1930s and early 1940s. But to be the most professional poet in the world is not in any sense to be the best; and Auden is using this extraordinary skill in managing a sadly reduced income. The power and emotion behind the poems, the incandescence of imagination, the pure drive of making, have become sadly diminished. There is a terrible tiredness and flatness about most of *Nones*, and this gives the skill and accuracy and sincerity of the best poems a lowly disquieting ring. There is a real pathos to the fact that the man who published *Poems* and *Paid on Both Sides* in 1930 as a boy of twenty-three, is publishing *Nones* in 1951 as a man of forty-four.[33]

Several times, Auden in *Nones*, begins a poem extremely well, develops it for a while, and then simply trails away, as if the effort of imagining, of making, were too exhausting; he seems always about to lapse into a state of just sitting on the bed and staring out the window—and then yawning. How he *used* facts, once—a fact came out of Auden looking as if it had been through an egg beater. How often, now, he *consents to* facts—presents them for what they are and lets it go at that: he's not arguing with you, he's telling you—there it is to see. This has produced some of the best and quietest and most truthful of the poems, but it has also produced some extremely flat, offhand, ordinary, methodical poems. Quite a few of the poems are trivial from the start: and quite a few are—to put it mildly—Familiar Types to the Auden reader, who beat the poet to the finish line by at least a head.

Yet one of these familiar patented poems, a poem recognizable as an Auden poem at a distance of ten miles in good weather, a poem describing the classical world in the most effectively anachronistic, modernistic terms, is so beautifully organized, imagined, realized, stands for so much, with such concentrated elegance, that few readers could repeat it without a surge of delight, without admitting, "Yes, say what you please about him, he *can* be magical." I'm referring [to] that little poem "The Fall of Rome," which I'll read to you.[34]

[Reads "The Fall of Rome."]

But two of the other poems in *Nones* surprised me as much as I've been surprised by a poem in several years. If you see a poem named "The Chimeras," that begins

> Absence of heart—as in public buildings,
> Absence of mind—as in public speeches,
> Absence of worth—as in goods intended for the public,
>
> Are telltale signs that a chimaera has just dined
> On someone else; of him, poor foolish fellow,
> Not a scrap is left, not even his name.
>
> Indescribable—being neither this nor that,
> Uncountable—being any number—
> Unreal—being anything but what they are.[35]

If you see such a poem, what *can* you say except, "Ah, Graves, poor dear Robert Graves! Inimitable, isn't he?" It's quite a nice Graves poem, too, both in form and content—not as characteristic as some, but more characteristic than others. And, three poems further along, the reader comes to a poem called "A Household," one that begins:

> When, to disarm suspicious minds at lunch
> Before coming to the point or at golf,
> The bargain driven, to soothe hurt feelings,
>
> He talks about his home, he never speaks

(A reticence for which they all admire him)
Of his bride so worshipped and so early lost,

But proudly tells of that young scamp his heir,
Of black eyes given and received, thrashings
Endured without a sound to save a chum;

Or calls their spotted maleness to revere
His saintly mother, calm and kind and wise,
A grand old lady pouring out the tea.

Whom, though, has he ever asked for the week-end?
Out to his country mansion in the evening,
Another merger signed, he drives alone:

To be avoided by a miserable runt
Who wets his bed and cannot throw or whistle,
A tell-tale, a crybaby, a failure;

To the revilings of a slatternly hag
Who caches bottles in her mattress, spits
And shouts obscenities from the landing;

Worse, to find both in an unholy alliance,
Youth stealing Age the liquor-cupboard key,
Age teaching Youth to lie with a straight face.[36]

This is quite a good Graves poem, too; if you know his poetry well, it's unmistakable, I think. But how extraordinary that *Auden* should have written them both. I'm not bringing this up as something against Auden, so that you'll say, "*Another* influence! Deplorable, deplorable!" This is one of the most interesting poetic phenomena of any experience: these are real poems, successful poems, conceived and worked out in detail, most of the time as Graves would have worked them out a few years ago—for once Auden is not merely taking what he wants from another writer, and using it as he pleases, but is getting to the heart of the matter and being transformed. No reviewer has said a word about these poems: this shows not only that reviewers don't know Graves's poetry very well, but it shows

even more interestingly how much Auden's poetry has changed—
put those two poems down into the middle of *On This Island* or *An-
other Time*, and they would stand out like two fried eggs.[37]

But most of the poems in *Nones* are recognizable and inimitably
Auden's, and half of them are either good or else good enough to
make our reading of them a real pleasure and our regret that they
aren't a *little* better a real regret—it would be a pleasure to read and
comment on such interesting poems as "The Managers," "Ischia,"
the first section of "Memorial for the City." At last a quieter good-
ness has grown up inside the immediately accessible, highly rhetor-
ical—sometimes frivolous, sometimes sermonish, sometimes very
thin, sometimes, however, beautifully successful—poetry that Au-
den had written for so many years, that had replaced the stranger,
tougher, stronger, less immediately accessible poetry of his early
years; and Auden has become capable, by a queer dry mocking ex-
aggeration of his more characteristic and elaborate rhetoric, of mak-
ing an interesting original, and successful use of it. A poem like "Un-
der Sirius" represents the happy disenchanted old age of the
rhetorician, when he realizes that it is by admitting the exaggera-
tion of his rhetoric, by using it as a tone he and the reader both
smile at, that he can use it to express his truth. A less successful
poem like "The Duet" represents the same process. The subject of
one of Frost's poems is a bird whose call, "All but frames in words"
the question: "What to make of a diminished thing?"[38] Auden's last
book shows us what *can* be made of a diminished thing: his gift, his
talents, do not seem to have the emotional intensity, the magical
transfiguring originality, that they had at one time, but sometimes
he has used them so well, with so much skill, intelligence, and dis-
abused sincerity, that they have produced some thoughtful, honest,
and successful poems.

I should like to finish my lecture by reading to you "Under Sirius."[39]

Lecture 5

There are three stages of the works—and of the ideas which are their sources or elaborated by-products—that we call Auden. In the beginning there is the Old Auden the *Ur*-Auden. For this stage many titles suggest themselves: *Freud and Grettir; Ontogeny Recapitulates Phylogeny; The Law of the Members.* An obvious and somewhat ambiguous motto for the stage would [be] Goethe's "What you have inherited from your fathers you must earn in order to possess"; almost as good would be Auden's own "We are lived by powers we pretend to understand," or the statement of Groddeck's from which Auden's line was derived: "We are 'lived' by unknown and uncontrollable forces."[1]

Here in this first stage everything happens inside the realm of causal or magical necessity. Here—in *Poems*, in *Paid on Both Sides*, and to a lesser degree in *The Orators*—is the world of the unconscious, the primitive, the childish, the animal, the natural: in the book of Auden this is Genesis. The basic logical picture underlying these poems is that of the long struggle of genetic development, of the hard, blind journey of the creature or its kind. Existence is an essentially dialectical evolution, presented with particular directness in Freudian or saga terms—i.e., in terms succeeding or preceding those of the higher religions. The primary subject of the poems is the discontinuities of growth, the unrecognized or opposed Necessity that determines men and Man: Hegel's critical points at which quantity changes into quality are nowhere else in literature so dramatically and movingly embodied. (We realize for the first time that these are, so to speak, great *problems* to the entity doing the changing; that the pan of water, before it finally becomes ice, is so full of a neurotic dread of its future, of a neurotic yearning to regress to its original gaseous state, that the whole thing seems to *it* a nervous breakdown.) In these early poems the "change of heart" is valueless except as a preliminary to change—is, often, an evasion by which we avoid changing. But even the real choices, the continued-in changes, have a deterministic pathos. Our fundamental activity is a guilty revolt against a guilty authority, a revolt predetermined to immediate or eventual failure, a revolt by the neurotic and diseased (to the Auden of Stage I medicine is a branch of psychiatry and all illness is functional) against a neurotic and diseased culture.

In Stage I morality is never the instant of choosing, but the years of doing. It is thought of not as a choice, a simple single act of the will, but as a long and almost impossibly difficult series of actions, a process of processes. True development—that is, genuinely moral behavior—has nothing to do with the systematic disinterested abstractions of the moralist; it is a labyrinth in which you yourself are trapped, a puzzle you work at all your life, failing or succeeding only to fail. This is a narrative morality instead of a sermon morality; morality as particular, experienced practice instead of morality as general, vicarious theory; Job's morality instead of that of his comforters. This morality of an endangered and uneasy participant speaking to himself is the opposite of the morality that succeeded it, when Auden spoke as a group adviser, with elevated, abstract, and sentimental understanding, to a group that had in common with him only its own confusion and good-heartedness. But morality, in the earliest Auden, is first of all a matter of self-development. To thine own potential self be true, the poems tell their readers, and both feel that *How shall a man make actual this potentiality?* is the essential problem, the essential difficulty, of morality. The poems are not able to trust in the golden rule or the categorical imperative or anything like them, since following those would necessitate giving in to the Father and, worse still, to the Mother—would necessitate a corrupt and acquiescent regression to an already-established state of things. (Regression *is* sin, in the earliest Auden.)

These early poems effect a strange assimilation of machinery and the industrial world into a traditional, rural, almost feudal world; the new world-view of an expanding, industrial, technological optimism rots away—as its machines rust to a halt, as its industry grinds down to perpetually lower and poorer levels—into the cyclic pessimism of an older view, the peasant pessimism which is the other face of the optimistic fantasy of the *Märchen*. The weight and concentration of the poems fall upon things (and those great things, animals and people) in their final plainness; these have kept the stolid and dangerous inertia of the objects of the sagas—the sword that snaps, the man looking at his lopped-off leg and saying, "That was a good stroke." The poems gain an uncommon plausibility from the terse, understated matter-of-factness of their treatment, the insistence (such as that found in the speech of children, in Mother Goose, in folk or savage verse, in dreams) that the words themselves are things. The objects of the poems are vaguely tabooish, totemistic, animistic—everything is full of *mana*, especially the machines, rusting tutelary deities of the countryside in which everything occurs: if Jung had had the early Auden as a patient he would have decided that rusting machines in the country are Archetypal Images of the Racial Unconscious. Auden's early style is rooted in the English countryside; his later style, compared to it, is an airplant in a window-box of the cloud-city of the *Wandervögel*. The early poems are in harmony with the more primitive levels of our experience, levels which—since they precede others in the life of the individual consciousness—underlie the moralistic and rationalizing levels at which the later Auden usually is working. When we say that some patch of an early poem seems "magical," we mean, sometimes, that the effect does not appear to be produced by any of the rhetorical devices we expect to find; that the poem works directly at levels which we are not accustomed to verbalize or scrutinize, often because they are taken for granted. These primitive levels of response of course persist in everybody, though suppressed, sublimated, or tacitly ignored by all manners. But in our culture how much (like the flaying of Marsyas) goes on under—far under—the level grey gaze of Reason and Taste; just as Apollo, when he was not occupied with knowledge, art, and light, slithered under the pillars of his temples in the person of a hunting snake, and was called by his worshippers the Mouse-Slayer.

In *On This Island* and *The Dog Beneath the Skin* Auden changes over into a second, essentially transitional stage which continues until *New Year Letter*, itself a transition from the Moral Auden to the New Auden. It is easy to find titles or mottoes for this second stage: *The Moralist from the Machine; The Questing Beast; Reason as Agape*, or *The Saviour with the Vote*. Here everything of importance happens in the realm of logical or ethical necessity.[2] Here we are free to choose— are implored or forced to choose, are told again and again that our choices are meaningful, that the right choice is predestined to success. A change of heart is a change of vote: what is meaningless about *that?* Existence itself has become a problem which Auden reasons about, advises us about, exhorts us to make the right choice about; it is categorized, rather than presented, in secular, liberal, humanitarian, sentimental, metaphorically scientific terms. The typical poems are problem poems. The political moralist raids a generalized, popularized science for the raw materials and imagery of a morality which he constructs to satisfy the demands of the self and of the age, but which he implies is scientific: a favorable mutation becomes for him "a morally good act," and even Destiny "presents itself in political terms," to be voted for or spoken against.[3] Animals, misguided former voters bogged down in the partial but final solutions brought them by their wasted votes, are rather patronizingly condemned by the political adviser because they are not free, like us, to go on voting (and being advised). Auden's ethics appear in an abstract, virtuous, and interminable Volume II, all the particulars of which are derived from a Volume I that consists of a single sentence: "We must do something about Hitler." We are all guilty, the will itself is evil (this judgment is a bitter pill with a sugar-and-morphine center); but we can, practically speaking, escape our guilt by recognizing it, by willing a sort of Popular Front of the universe. The quoted *Freedom is the recognition of necessity* (originally, in the purely deterministic Spinoza, the recognition that there is no freedom except the "freedom" of acting according to the conditions of our being, of knowing and consequently loving the universe we cannot even wish to change) has developed, through the growingly optimistic determinism of Hegel and Engels, into Auden's consolatory fable: *To recognize necessity is to have escaped it.*[4] Thus the fundamental logical picture underneath the poems is that of the fairy tale quest (and the assimilated quest of the Grail, temptations of the Buddha or the Messiah, and so forth): so much so that genetic development, the underlying logical picture of the first stage, is itself expressed in terms of the quest. Success is no longer struggled for interminably and found at last a failure, but is won, in an instant, by choosing correctly—i.e., voting. Good will *is* Grace: in this ideally democratic fable the third son—a humble and unexceptional hero distinguished from his able and eager brothers by his amorphous generalization, his foetalization—tramps goodheartedly and selflessly over the conditions of the universe, choosing, choosing, up to a final choice; a choice rewarded by an external, causally unrelated, paradoxical "success." Actually his normal state is its own reward, his real reward: "Success" is merely the morphological stamp of approval necessary to impress the undiscerning hearers of the parable; it is truly success only insofar as it resembles the state it rewards. Thus the third son, in his most developed and Audenish, his truest form, sits happily at home, already successful, and reads with indifference the love-letters of his more primitive forebear, trudging unnecessarily over the tundra. The Pole was in his backyard all the time.

There is only one real name for Auden's third period, from 1940–46 or '47: *Paul*; but one is tempted by *Grace Abounding; The Teleological Suspension of Ethics; Waiting for the Spark from Heaven to Fall.* Here everything that is important happens in the realm of Grace. The fundamental logical picture underlying the poems is that of waiting

humbly for Grace; man's ultimate accomplishment is sitting still. We
are damned not merely for what we do, but for doing anything at
all—and properly damned, for what *we* do is necessarily evil: *Do not,
till ye be done for* is our only possible slogan. In Stage II action and the
will were evil, but in Stage III everything (except the Wholly Oth-
er, God) is evil; for Auden, like Niebuhr, accepts the Fall not mere-
ly as a causal myth, but as the observed essence of all experience.[5]
But the speeches no longer support any Universal Popular Front.
Who are we to help out God's World? (Better wait it out instead.)
The earlier "We must do something about Hitler" has become "We
must realize we ARE Hitler." There is no more choice—we are cho-
sen; the elections of the free voter, the man of good will and good
works, have been succeeded by the Election of the helpless and de-
termined sinner, the man of faith. The whole concept of evolution-
ary development has disappeared. The old Adam of the flesh (blind-
ed by self-love, self-righteousness, and self-conceit pumped into
him by the secular intelligence, the wisdom of this world) must mu-
tate into the New Adam of the spirit. Just as natural mutations are,
often, the effects of extra-terrestrial radiation, this supernatural mu-
tation is an effect or aspect of the unearthly radiation of Grace—
that is, it *is* Grace as it feels to us who receive it. (After making up
this rather derisive simile, I was astonished to find Auden, in some-
thing I hadn't read before, using it seriously: Agape is "Eros mutat-
ed by Grace.")[6] The change of heart and its accompanying changes
of behavior are now important only as a sign that we have been
changed, elected—just as they were in Calvin; but the implacable
confidence of the theocrat (once re-created for our age, in an un-
precedented feat of the historic imagination, by Karl Barth) has
scaled away, exposing its shaky armature of guilt and hope.[7] The
determinism of Stage I has returned, but transfigured by that Chris-
tian optimism which, in its avid acceptance of the worst evils of our
world as inseparable from fleshly existence, is more frightening than
the most pessimistic of secular views. This already determined text
of existence is neither presented, as in Stage I; nor categorized, as
in Stage II; but commented on. Auden's work begins to consist of
commentaries or glosses of every kind—dramatic, philosophical,

critical. He becomes fond of writing criticisms or reviews which, under a vague or dutiful show of criticizing a work some magazine has hopefully handed him, are secondary commentaries or glosses on those primary commentaries or glosses which are his creative works (so that readers of his reviews are continually exclaiming, "Now I see!"). These primary and secondary glosses are indistinguishable in dialectic and imagery—purple patches, heartfelt confessions, and memorable feats of dialectical ingenuity reach their highest concentration in reviews of minor theologians.

In this stage Auden has not forsaken ethics—how could so confirmed a moralist? But his morals are now, like the Law in Luther or Niebuhr, merely a crutch with which to beat us into submission, to force home to us the realization that there is none good but God, that no works can either save us or make us worth saving. The Old Auden he has been forced to forget entirely—just as, in Freud's account of us, we are forced to wipe from our conscious memories all the experiences of our earliest childhood. (In his *Collected Poetry* Auden makes extensive changes in the poems of Stage II, but either omits the poems of Stage I or leaves them unchanged—they are so genuinely and completely alien to him that he can do nothing with them. To prove that he neither understands nor sympathizes with his earliest work, he destroys *Paid on Both Sides* by following Untermeyer's precedent of printing a number of fragments as lyrics.[8] Yet he does seem to have kept a queer superstitious respect for his earliest poems, since he reprints most of them, and omits a far greater proportion of the poems from *On this Island*.) But the Secular Auden of Stage II is the New Auden's favorite target of attack. Herod—hitherto represented by everybody as an aboriginal ogre, Freud's father of the primal horde—is presented in "For the Time Being" as the humane, secular, liberal Auden of Stage II. This explains the fervid rudeness of the attack: Auden is attempting to get rid of the stumbling block of a dead self by chopping it up and dropping the pieces into quicklime. Why should anyone represent *Herod* as the typical liberal? It would have been far more natural and far more plausible to pick Pontius Pilate (at that time the only regular subscriber to the *Nation* in all Palestine): but Auden could not risk the sympathy for Pilate which, increasingly injected into the gospels as they developed—as anti-Semitic propaganda, incidentally—has been inherited by all of us. We are so used to rejecting Herod as a particularly bogey-ish Churchill that Auden can count on our going right on rejecting him when he is presented as Attlee.[9]

But under all the changing surface forms of Auden's develop-ment—often almost grotesquely at variance with one another—there is a constellation of a few persistent organizing forces. The ex-amination of these is a key to the understanding of the surface changes, of the development itself; particularly if we realize that in development the opposite of an attitude is often more immediately allied to it than any intermediate position is—and that Auden's ra-tionalizations of his changes, however irrational they may seem, should rarely be considered of *causal* importance.[10]

A complex of ideas, emotions, and unconscious attitudes about anxiety, guilt, and isolation—fused or not yet separated in a sort of sexual-authoritarian matrix—is the permanent causal core of Auden's ideology. It is structural and basic in his nature; compared to it most other things are skin or hair, the mere bloom of rouge. In Auden's work these elements of *anxiety, guilt, isolation, sexuality,* and *authority* make up a true gestalt, a connected and meaningful whole; but the necessities of analysis force the analyst to sketch them one by one, as they appear in the successive stages of Auden's development.

In Stage I *guilt* is ubiquitous, since (a) from his Freudian point of view all levels can be reduced to lower, genetically prior levels—"re-ally" are "nothing but" these discreditable animal, savage, or infan-tile levels; since (b) from his dialectical-evolutionary, formally if vaguely Hegelian point of view, any success or good is temporary, already beginning to assume its permanent, discredited, and guilty status of failure or evil; since (c) if we look either through Freud's or Marx's eyes, our "reasons" for doing anything never except by rare chance coincide with the "real," less creditable reasons, so that our whole rational life is adulterated by the guilty hypocrisy of our half-diseased, half-insane rationalization or ideology. ("Ideology is a process which of course is carried on with the consciousness of the so-called thinkers, but with a false consciousness. The real driving force which moves it remains unconscious, otherwise there would be no ideology." This description of what we should call rationalization appeared in the *Anti-Dühring* in 1878.)[11]

Choice, will itself, Auden thinks of as a "necessary error": whatever we do is wrong, inadequate, done for reasons we do not understand, so that we are never free of either guilt or *anxiety*. To a more or less rational anxiety is added sexual anxiety, that of repressed or forbidden sexual development; genetic anxiety, that of the creature which can neither grow nor evolve properly, whose most spectacular success is never anything more than a specialized and exaggerated impasse from which it is now too late to escape; moral anxiety—for in the early Auden the superego is as strong as it is confused, and he finds it difficult, though imperative, either to know what he should do or to find out how to do it; and hypochondriacal, neurotic anxiety, both psychic and somatic—in "this country of ours where nobody is well," even diseases normally considered organic are something that we *mean* (see Groddeck), so that our hypochondriacal anxiety is a guilty one as well.[12]

In Stage I Auden is guiltily and partially rejecting, revolting against, *authority*. That part of us which does not revolt, judged either by reason or by our own conscious standards, is despicable in its neurotic or diseased, bourgeois, corruptly passive guilt; but that part of us which revolts against the authority of the Father and the State is guilty by *their* standards, our own unconscious standards: so much so that it desperately seeks sanction in the mythical authority of that hastily invented fiction the Uncle, our "real Ancestor." It is as if the gnawn and rock-bound Prometheus, in order to justify any future rebellion, had had to postulate a "real" Zeus and a "real" vulture under whose authority he "really" was. (And Prometheus, if he was not an orphan, may have felt compelled to do something of the sort: we all can remember how, in our own time, Little Father Nicholas has been replaced by Little Fathers Lenin and Stalin, Holy Russia by the Fatherland.) Auden's early apotheosis of the (Wicked) Uncle is no more than an innocent, Protestant, and Beatrix-Potterish form of diabolism. It is no surprise to learn, in *Letters from Iceland* and other places, that Auden's parents were unusually good ones, very much venerated by the child: Auden moralizes interminably, cannot question or reject Authority except under the aegis of this pathetically invented opposing authority, because the superego (or whatever term we wish to use for the mechanism of conscience and authority) is exceptionally strong in him—as Kardiner says, "The superego is based on affection, not hatred; on delegated and not enforced authority."[13] People have always been puzzled by the doom that hangs like a negative halo over the heads of the revolutionists of Auden's early works, who without exception commit suicide, die, or fail. But Auden *must* reward them only with failure or death, in order to relieve the guilt of his own revolt; those who defy Authority must come to bad ends, he knows, and he their creator has at least made them come to such ends, thus satisfying Authority at the same time he has revolted against it. This helps to explain, among other things, Auden's making his revolutionists as neurotic and diseased as the diseased and neurotic society they revolt against. But one should notice that he uses dadaist and surrealist elements primarily as symptoms; the rather comic (and essentially Catholic) life-cycle of the French surrealists—who die at advanced ages, prosperous, well-adjusted, and still surrealists—is inconceivable to Auden, the product of a moralistic and Protestant culture.

In Stage I guilt is particularly apparent in connection with *sexuality*, a sexuality repressed and condemned by both external and internal authority. This sexuality seems disease like so much else, revolt like so much else: the lover is presented as the leader of a secret cult, as the revolutionist, as the growing organism seduced into regression, but most of all as the sick neurotic—we are given so many lists of the fetishes of abnormal and difficult sexuality that we tend to believe a normal or easy sort not only rare but nonexistent. Love is condemned by the Immanent Will within the evolving animal as a fatal, foetal regression, as the great refusal of the creature; when we love women—who are always, in these cases, the primary vessels of sexual wrath—we are giving in to the Mother, stagnating, corruptly acquiescing to Authority instead of persisting in the difficult revolution of growth. Even when treated most favorably love is considered something to be transcended, to be replaced by "independent delight"—it is an escape from which Auden would like to escape. In the psychoanalytical terms haunting Auden's head, it was nothing but oral, anal, or genital stages of drives which, dammed up, diverted, or finally breaking free in disguise, were always subjective, predetermined states superficially related to some objective pretext, rather than real responses to a person who is loved. Love is seen as a way of hysterically blinding ourselves to our own essential, unchanging isolation—as a sort of Ignoble Lie. (But Auden defends its excesses when other people attack them, by retorting that naturally they seem sick and distorted to a sick, distorted, capitalist world.) It would be hard to make a better summary of what underlies much of Auden's development than Kardiner's generalization of evidence gathered from several cultures: "If the exercise of sexuality falls under the influence of parental authority, all obedience constellations are reinforced, the parents' value for good or evil becomes exaggerated, and guilt about sexual activity leads to anticipation of punishment and the fear of success."[14] If this guilt is reinforced by society in later life, as it has been in Auden's case, the whole process is strengthened.

Auden has always insisted, with seemingly disproportionate violence, upon the essential and inexorable *isolation* of the individual; one can find dozens of different statements of the proposition. He usually states flatly that it's so, and that's all there is to it; you must *be* alone and realize that you are alone, like it or not—any argument or gregariousness is romantic and primitive wishful-thinking. This attitude, in Stage I, is grounded both in his genetic view of the individual organism (which is separately frustrated and separately liquidated, without exception, even if its species triumphs) and in his Freudian view of ontogenetic development as an unaccountably faithful recapitulation of phlyogenetic development. Some of his most beautiful poems express the terrifying and pathetic isolation of the growing organism, unwillingly alone from the moment it is thrust from the womb. He has been cut off from any real union with Authority by his revolt against it; and sexual relations, the next chance at "Togetherness," are to him no more than a predetermined, repetitively senseless process of isolated growth—the object of love is a mere external pretext, not essentially different from the class of abnormal fetishes of which it is, so to speak, the one normal member. The Family is gone. But if it, our culture's normal complex of togetherness, is broken up, both the feelings of isolation and the guilt feeling connected with sex are enormously intensified. This is particularly apparent in the case of such a writer as Hart Crane: his helpless rejection of the normal family, the normal sexual situation of union, isolated him both from his past and in his future—for he knew that he himself was never going to repeat this situation; and, in his present, what sexual ties he attempted had for him no trace of permanence, of acceptance by authority.

The hero of Stage I, the revolutionary cult leader—inadequately understood by his followers, entirely misunderstood by the rest of the world—is almost wholly isolated. The hero of *The Orators* resorts to political action of a fantastic sort—or, rather, to a fantasy of political action—which necessarily fails; and he ends by "understanding" that a complete submission to Authority is the only method of reforming Authority and saving himself: "God just loves us all, but *means to be obeyed* [my italics]."[15] It is no accident that this Airman is last seen several miles of cold air away from the nearest living creature, about to kill himself; and it is no wonder that the creator of this Airman, finally understanding the uselessness of his own political action in that Black Year which all earth knew, and trembled at—1940 in this case—should end up "floating over 70,000 fathoms," in utter submission to that Authority Who means to be obeyed, the God of Kierkegaard and Barth.[16] Laplace's Calculator might have predicted most of Auden's development from the last two pages of *The Orators*.[17] (Kierkegaard's phrase about seventy thousand fathoms attracted Auden so much that he adopted it as a disquieting slogan for our union with God—the only possible union, incidentally.)

In an approving summary of one existential point of view, Auden states that "the basic human problem is man's anxiety in time."[18] By the time Auden had arrived at Stage II his *anxiety* had begun to find expression as much in guilty activity as in passive guilt—it is the period of his most active anxiety, so far as politics and the "real world"

are concerned. Our decision is always *the* decision, the great divid-
ing watershed from which events fall to evil or to good: the crises
of existence come as regularly and hyperbolically as elections. This
political, liberal anxiety is rarely even temporarily soothed—since
everything went, everything always goes against the Popular Front;
the accompanying moral anxiety cannot be soothed, even tem-
porarily—since the means to the Best end is rarely even Good, since
acting with the best will in the world is still acting, since even the
purest contemplation is always on the verge of signing its eternal,
predestined pact with that "Hitlerian monster," the Will.

In Stage II *guilt* is first of all social, liberal, abstractly ethical
guilt—a guilt so general as to seem almost formal. It is we who are
responsible, either by commission or—more ordinarily—by omis-
sion, for everything from exterminating the Tasmanians to burning
the books at Alexandria. (You didn't do it? Then you should have
stopped them from doing it. You never hear of it? Ignorant as well
as evil, eh? You weren't born? You're guilty, I tell you—*guilty*.) Guilt
is used to beat us into an easy but active submission, that of the vot-
er, the signer of petitions, he who dies for freedom in the future the
vote and the signature have prevented. Yet we are told that if we
make up our minds, do anything, we are as guilty as before: for *all*
will, *all* action, are evil. (From this universal secular condemnation
it was easy for Auden to pass to Original Sin, the universal deprav-
ity of Calvinism.) Deep within the liberal—who feels that he *does*
less than he ought—nothing calms more profoundly, alleviates
more gratefully, the anxiety always gnawing at the core of his good-
heartedness, than the feeling of *group guilt*. What precarious individ-
ual acquittal can rival the "We are all guilty" that wipes out at one
stroke any specific, differentiation guilt of one's own? What propo-
sition can express more fully and more tactfully one's own sensibil-
ity and honesty? ("Look how guilty I feel over what most people
wouldn't even be bothered by. Most people think it's quite possible
to will or do something without being *necessarily* guilty.")[19]

Much of the guilt of Stage II is moral, the guilt the moralizer nec-
essarily ascribes to his backward moralizees. But much of it is a mat-
ter of *sexuality*. Love has come to be thought of as a guilty evasion,

an escape from actuality. To excuse itself it must "implicate" itself in society, politics, the "real world." Love is a station we stop at when we should go on with the train; a power or insight we selfishly bury, instead of using in the social situation. It *should* be sublimated in Social Service. Eros is—at least potentially—a secular, humanitarian Agape which we have perverted. Love is, before everything, a problem; the poor lover is part of a Corneillian struggle between love and his moral and political duty to the world. In this contest between public and private, objective and subjective, Paris always dutifully awards his prize—that golden word, *Real*—to Minerva, but not without one burning backward glance. Love is, like Iceland, "an island and therefore unreal." Later on Auden rewrote the line, changing *unreal* to *a refuge*, but in those days he knew, just as Hitler did, that *There are no more islands.*[20] But the *are* of this proposition, in Auden's case, was a normative judgment, not an existential judgment. Auden's uneasy disapproval of Love was grounded, partially, in society's disapproval, just as his interminable moralizing is: if his attitudes and behavior had been accepted by society without question he might have cared less about morality. As it was he needed, always, to be right, good, well-meaning—and he became a moral perfectionist of an odd and interesting order.

In Stage II Auden feels the reluctant *isolation* of the liberal intellectual of the late-capitalist state—the terrible aloneness of the Mediator who is neither flesh nor fowl, but poor pink herring. He sits among the ashes of his own doubts, waiting, waiting. But nobody comes to persuade the Persuader; the only ties left to him are the pale vicarious ties of voting, of petition-signing, of "the flat ephemeral pamphlet and the boring meeting."[21] Staring enviously at the iron orthodoxy of the Communists his allies, at the beefy certainty of the Tories his opponents, at the folkish and bloody oneness of the Fascists his enemies, he insists, with wistful desperation, that his own isolation is inescapable for everyone in the world; that the machine has made everyone understand "the secret that was *always* [my italics] true / But known once only to the few," the secret that "Aloneness is man's real condition."[22] He cries in a shaky voice, "I welcome the atomization of society"; and, in speaking of Kafka's heroes, states the Law of all modern life: "An industrial civilization makes *everyone* an exceptional reflective K."[23] (O Churchill! O Stalin! You *very* exceptional K.'s! What shall I say of this enchanting error, worthy of Peter Rabbit the day he first heard from his mother of the World of Mr. MacGregor?) This projection upon the universe of one's own self and situation, as the necessary law of that universe, is usual in Auden—and common enough in anyone . . . In Stage II his heroes are entirely alone: the false hero, the Extrinsically Successful One, wanders through the wilderness on the lonely quest that ends in an arbitrary and external success, completely misunderstood by the very public that applauds him; the real hero, the Intrinsically Successful One, potters about the garden at home, so completely alone that nobody in the world except the false hero even suspects that he is a success.

Auden's attitude toward *authority* has changed. In Stage I Auden had rebelled, though guiltily, against a guilty authority: he represented the new, potential good rejecting the old and hardened evil of an authority which had itself come into power by revolting against, killing, and eating an earlier authority (according to Freud's late-Victorian anthropological fantasy).[24] In Stage II Auden tries to reform the father, the state, authority; everyone concerned has become less guilty, and Auden's method of operation is now to persuade authority into a recognition of its essential goodheartedness, into a reconciliation with himself and with the Reason which is over all things, gods and men alike. His relation to authority is notably ambivalent—naturally so, since the relation is that of reform. A certain childishness (not too rare in young English intellectuals, who are sheltered and cherished in comparison with our own Wild Boys) becomes apparent in his attitudes—I remember a reviewer's talking of the "typical boyish charm" of the Auden poem of this period, and Auden complained that all his friends complained, "Why doesn't Wystan ever grow up?"[25] (He doesn't repeat the magical answer he must have made: "All children, except one, grow up.") Auden is managing to stay on surprisingly good terms with authority by assuming the role of *enfant terrible* of the reformers—a very goodhearted and very childish one, the *enfant terrible* of the old father's long soft summer dreams. He becomes fond of saying that his favorite writers, those he would like most to *be*, are Lear, Carroll, and the author of *Peter Rabbit*—who themselves (as Auden remembers nostalgically) reformed or rejected society in their ways, though not in any ways that kept them out of the nicest nurseries. Of course much of the appeal of his statement, to Auden, lay in its shock value; but he could have dismayed his readers quite as heartily by telling them that his favorite writers were Tarski and Frege.[26] His admiration was genuine.

In Stage II Auden nourishes a residual, partially perverse affection for any maladjustment to society, for any complex or neurosis his development may have left lying around in him: after all, authority itself, in the process of reform, has to adjust itself a little to poor ill-adjusted me. He is an unreconstructed liberal who feels an uneasy but thorough dislike for that "goddess of bossy underlings, Normality," and all the nursery schools and feeding-formulas that follow in her train; he betrays an astonishing repugnance to such concomitants of Progress as antisepsis and central heating, prays *Preserve me from the Shape of Things to Be*, and invents as *his* educational slogan: "Let each child have that's in our care / As much neurosis as the child can bear."[27] The ideal education is "manual labor and Greek." Cassandra and every other foreign slave in Hellas could have cheered themselves with the reflection that at least they were going to get an ideal education. But could any Greek—who, after all, already *knew* Greek—have received an ideal education?[28] Auden's position has its difficulties. But all this thrusting-out of the lips only corresponds to the petulance with which Alice, an eminently reasonable child, greeted any divergence of Wonderland from one's own household's routine—which *is* Reason. Besides, Auden is reacting against his earlier Groddeck-Lane period; and since he is being unusually good and thoughtful so far as society is concerned, he feels it only fair for society to take as lenient a view as possible of any neuroses *he* can bear. But Auden's ideology, at any stage, seems unconsciously but specifically designed to leave its creator intact.

But later on, in Stage III of his development, Auden repudiates with fear and revulsion any attempt to revolt against Authority, to reform Authority, to question Authority, or to remain independent of Authority in any way. Such an attempt is an insane depravity that is the root of all sin. He knows that—as Kierkegaard puts it in his wonderful, if unintentional, eight-word summary of Calvinism—"The only thing which interests God is obedience."[29] (This is lucky since, if Calvin's right, it is all that He gets.) But Auden is no Calvin—no logician, either, in this particular case—and he tactfully overlooks any direct hand of the Creator in His creature's guilt. The only responsibility that Auden, as a representative neurotic theologian, does not thankfully delegate to God is the responsibility for his own guilty depravity. *That* he is responsible for, he confesses—with the abject, appealing leer of Peter Lorre in *M*—but everything else in the universe God is responsible for. This satisfies at one stroke Auden's anxiety (he is assured that he can and should do nothing himself); his need for guilt and his need to be reconciled to that guilt; and his need of an inexorable and unconditioned Authority.

When we have constructed God as the Wholly Other than ourselves who are wholly evil; when we have decreed that the image of God has been "wholly blotted out" in many by the Fall, we naturally find the problem of mediation between the Wholly Other and that which it is wholly other than, a logically insoluble problem. We *require*—that is, we have made ourselves require—a self-contradictory, paradoxical, absurd mediator. Authority is now considered to be absolutely unconditioned, at once the Everything and the Not-Everything: shall *we* attempt to depose or limit God by demanding that he accord with our morality, our reason, or anything else that we possess? The demands of Authority are equally unconditioned. But our own troubling actual existence wholly disappears in our believing, vicarious identification with Authority. Fortunate circumstance! Since that existence is wholly evil: as Luther says, "In every good work the just man sins."[30] Or, as Auden puts it, in every act we "do / Evil as each creature does / In every definite decision / To improve; for even in / The germ-cell's primary division / Innocence is lost and sin, / Already given as a fact, / Once more issues as an act."[31] If Luther had only known about that germ-cell's primary division! The advances of science have almost enabled Auden to beat

Luther and Calvin at their own game. But they were handicapped by taking it more seriously. The later Auden is rarely serious: he is either solemn or ingeniously frivolous, like some massive and labyrinthine town-clock from which a corked Topsy and a gilt Eva somersault to mark the hours of Time, but from which Uncle Tom himself, rattling the keys and surrounded by the flames of Judgment, emerges to herald the advent of Eternity.

The Buddha said that he taught nothing but suffering and the escape from suffering; Auden, during most of the 1940s, could say that he taught nothing but guilt, *which is* the escape from guilt. To be able to spend his time feeling guilty over the primary fission of the germ-cell, and to regard as a negligible corollary of it that primary fission of the atom which produced in a few minutes several hundred thousand casualties—what a God-sent mercy this ability is to anyone, what an expression of the depths and necessities of his being! What escape from responsibility or from guilt can equal this responsibility, this guilt? Is not the death of these poor guilty creatures—damned as they were by their lack of any connection with God through the one Mediator, Christ—only one more relatively unimportant effect of that first Fall which transformed every succeeding action of man into a guilty horror? How unimportant these inevitably trivial secular issues must seem to the man to whom God has brought it home that there is only *one* issue: the obedience of the guilty soul to God, the soul's salvation by the grace of God.[32]

Over and over Auden attacks every "good" act, every attempt to "improve." He reiterates that "it is not enough to bear witness [i.e., to be a martyr] for even protest is wrong."[33] He writes, with that overweening humility which is the badge of all his saints, the humility of Luther, Calvin, Kierkegaard, and Barth: "Convict our pride of its offense / In all things, even penitence."[34] So far as this sort of penitence is concerned, it is impossible to resist his contention. When we look at the world around us and within us, and then think of a statement like Niebuhr's, that only rebellion against God "is sin in the strictest sense of the word," it is bitter not to be allowed to include the statement itself within the category of "sin in the strictest sense of the word."[35] But I am applying ethical concepts to a realm in which, as the most casual witness must have observed, all ordinary ethics is suspended.

Auden first slipped in to this dark realm of Faerie (this "horrible nightmare" of Calvinism, as the goaded Froude confessed) on the furtive excursions of the unbeliever who needs some fake photographs of the Little People for a new edition of *Peter Pan*, but who ends up as a cook's boy helping the gloomier dwarfs boil toads and snails, in preparation for the love-feast that celebrates the consummation of their mysteries. Thus in *New Year Letter* many things are used as mere metaphors or conceits which a few months later are accepted as dogmatic and eternal truths. For instance, in it the status of the Devil (who has "no positive existence," but who nonetheless perpetually pushes us over into Good) is still exactly that of A. A. Milne's bears which eat you if you step on the cracks in the pavement—lovable hypostatized fictions of the pragmatic moralist. But I have no doubt that Christopher Robin, after a few years of avoiding cracks, used to wake screaming from a recurrent dream that he had been swallowed by a bear; and Auden before long was living in such a dream.

In Stage III Auden no longer feels so much anxiety about *sexuality*, after he has filed it away under Religion; even its guilt is lost in the guilt of that universal depravity which has rolled its black flood over every human action. And Eros, considered as the not-yet-mutated Agape into which Agape is always relapsing, has gained a new respectability; it is Grandmother, who was not everything she might have been, but who left us all the money for the Asylum. Sexuality is now no more than a relatively minor aspect of our religious life. Auden explains, in a summary of Kierkegaard, that for the individual once exposed to Christianity—whether or not he believes—there are only three possibilities: marriage, celibacy, or despair. Now all three of these possibilities are religious states, relations which involve both man and God: sexuality is swallowed up in salvation—or, worse, damnation. One is not sure which of these possibilities Auden thinks of as his own state; probably he, as usual, considers all three "aspects of one Reality," and thus can credit himself with one-third of each. (This is an extravagant but by no means impossible suggestion: Auden's favorite method of mediating between irreconcilables is to declare them "merely aspects" of one reality, a reality that turns out to be as self-contradictory, absurd, and finally unsearchable as the ways of God.)

In Stage III Auden is completely alone, but the knowledge of his *isolation* is not a burden but a blessing: he knows that we have always been alone, will always be alone, except in our paradoxical union with the Wholly Other, God; and he knows that he is fortunate not to be blinded by illusions of any impossible union with the creatures, rather than with their Creator. Our isolation is the complete aloneness of the man who stands for every minute of his life, in fear and trembling and abject dread, before his God. One could describe this isolation with authoritative immediacy by quoting or paraphrasing the pages of Kierkegaard and Kafka from which Auden derives all of the spirit and much of the letter of his treatment. Few of the ideas of Auden's last stage have any novelty to a reader acquainted with Luther, Calvin, and Barth; the expression of most of the ideas has little novelty to a reader familiar with Kierkegaard and Kafka. But this is a Godsend for everybody concerned, since the theological ideas which Auden does not adopt but invents are all too often on the level of those brown paper parcels, brought secretly to the War Department in times of national emergency, which turn out to be full of plans to destroy enemy submarines by tracking them down with seals.

A more radical *anxiety* has transformed the solutions of Stage II into *what we are anxious about* in Stage III: we are resignedly, humbly, interminably anxious about everything but God. What is not anxious *is* God, His Grace; though even that is agonizingly conscious, every instant, of those seventy thousand fathoms over which it is precariously floating, trying desperately not even to wiggle its toes. What we are most anxious about is our anxiety itself: the greatest of all sins, Auden learns from Kafka, is impatience—and he decides that the hero "is, in fact, one who is not anxious."[36] But it was inevitable that Auden should arrive at this point. His anxiety is fundamental; and the one thing that anxiety cannot do is to accept itself, to do nothing about itself—consequently it admires more than anything else in the world doing nothing, sitting still, waiting.

In Stages I and II *success* is important as the opposite of (hence, the goal of) the organism's core of anxiety, guilt, and isolation. In Auden's last stage success is naturally replaced by salvation, since Auden is running the Time-Machine in reverse, exhibiting the familiar development of Western man backwards.

In Stage I success is something we are struggling for, developing into; it is unsatisfactory except as a goal—attained, it is seen as the failure forward from which we struggle, backward to which we regress. The Successful One is the revolutionary cult-leader who dies, the evolving qualitative leap that is in its turn superseded.

In Stage II success splits into extrinsic and intrinsic success. Extrinsic success is altogether externalized, something we earn by the arbitrary process of choosing, voting, making the lucky guess predestined to success. This extrinsic success is nothing more than the lucky charm, the Sacred Object of the fairy-tale quests—which you can have but never, alas! be. (Auden, spectacularly—and to himself guiltily—successful, realizes without any trouble that something is wrong with this sort of extrinsic success, that not one thing is solved for him by it: after all, you can believe that success is going to change everything for you only so long as you have not been successful.) The Extrinsically Successful One is understood, forgivingly but rather contemptuously, to be a pathetic sham. Intrinsic success is entirely internalized, introjected: its humble, commonplace, and apparently wholly unsuccessful Successful One is all being and no doing. His success is, precisely, salvation without God, a secular salvation that seems necessarily and fatally incomplete without the divine ground from which it sprang. This intrinsic success is humble enough for Authority not to punish it except by a complete lack of recognition.

One passage from Freud fits Auden's attitudes toward guilt, Authority, and success, his whole development, so well that I should like to quote it here:

> When first the super-ego is set up there is no doubt that the function is endowed with that part of the child's aggressiveness against its parents for which it can find no discharge outwards on account of its

love-fixation and external difficulties; and, for this reason, the sever-
ity of the super-ego need not correspond to the severity of its up-
bringing. It is quite likely that when on subsequent occasions ag-
gressiveness is suppressed, the instinct follows the path [i.e., the path
inward] which was opened to it at that decisive period. People in
whom this unconscious sense of guilt is dominant, distinguish them-
selves under analytic treatment by exhibiting what is so unwelcome
from the point of view of prognosis—a negative therapeutic reac-
tion. In the normal course of events, if one gives a patient the solu-
tion of a symptom, at least the temporary disappearance of that
symptom should result; with these patients, on the contrary, the ef-
fect is a momentary intensification of the symptom and the suffering
that accompanies it. . . . Their behavior will appear as an expression
of an unconscious sense of guilt, which favors illness with its atten-
dant sufferings and handicaps.

And, Freud goes on to say, this unconscious need for punishment
"behaves like a part of the conscience, like the prolongation of con-
science into the unconscious."[37]

In Stage III success (always feared and distrusted because of its el-
ement of revolt, independence, separateness) is seen to be impossi-
ble. Intrinsic success becomes religious salvation, Grace—and its
passivity and determinism come to seem less arbitrary; extrinsic suc-
cess is realized to be one of the more important varieties of sin, a
variety particularly characteristic of scientific, industrial, secular
man. Influenced by Kafka's meditation on psychoanalysis, Auden
states that "half our troubles, both individual neuroses and collec-
tive manias like nationalism, seem to be caused largely by our
poverty of symbols, so that not only do we fail to relate one expe-
rience to another but also we have to entrust our whole emotional
life to the few symbols we do have."[38] This is penetrating as intro-
spection; but though it is true that the great organizing symbols, the
determiners of Auden's development, are few, he is perfectly well
able to relate *any* experience to any other experience, since the re-
lation can be as superficial and paradoxical—as absurd—as he pleas-
es. It is this which makes it difficult for him to learn something in

the full sense of *learn*: when we learn and assert A we cannot con-
tinue to assert not-A; but this Auden not only does, but knows that
he is required to do——not to do so, as he states again and again, is
a great sin, that sin by which Adam fell: "He could only eat of the
Tree of Knowledge of Good and Evil by forgetting that its existence
was a fiction of the Evil One, that there is only the Tree of Life."[39]
Nothing is good or bad but thinking makes it so (i.e., makes it seem
so): this is an old song—there is a beautiful version of it in
Herodotus—but it is rare to find it utilized in just this way by the
religious. Statements important to Auden often end with *There is only
ONE Something-or-other*, since there is nothing he admires so extrava-
gantly as monism, fears so superstitiously as dualism; yet his rhetor-
ical monism flowers from an absolute dualism that he has stated
only to transcend. The whole theological tradition Auden comes at
the tail of is essentially a series of adaptations of the dualism of Paul;
and as Auden, with the simplicity of genius, has understood, the
only practical and effective way of transforming it into monism is to
state that it has already been transformed. This Auden has done.

The stages of Auden's development can even be diagrammed. In
Stage I Anxiety and Guilt are fused in an Isolated, Sexual core, con-
sciously repelling or cowering under (and unconsciously attracting
or yearning up to) the authority that hangs in menacing ambiva-
lence overhead. In Stage II an active Anxiety dominates this core; it
has pushed Sexuality to the side as far as it can, and attempts rather
unsuccessfully to mitigate its confessed Guilt and Isolation by re-
forming the Authority it pulls down to it in Auden's traditional
Jacob-and-the-angel wrestling match. But in Stage III Anxiety,
Guilt, and Isolation are themselves the *relations* of Authority to the
core; they *are* Grace (its mirror-image, as Auden puts it), the means
by which Authority is manipulating the core into salvation. In this
stage Sexuality, mutated into Agape, is itself floating somewhere up
near God. The reader may complain about my last diagram: "But
what is left to be the core?" That is the point I was making: there is
nothing left. The one thing the Christian must realize is that he is
"less than any of God's creatures," that he is swallowed up in Au-
thority, the wholly determining Authority of God.

This was early plain to Auden. At about New Year, 1940, he dis-
approvingly judged that the Calvinist tradition makes man "the pas-
sive instrument of daemonic powers"; but by the anniversary of this
date, in the *Nation* of January 4, 1941, he was giving the theologian
Niebuhr (who in Cromwell's time would undoubtedly have been
named Death-on-Pride Niebuhr) a little neo-Calvinist lecture *á la*
Kierkegaard: he is "not sure" that Niebuhr "is sufficiently *ashamed* [*my
italics*]," mourns over Niebuhr's "orthodoxy," and ends by threaten-
ingly demanding that Niebuhr decide once and for all "whether he
believes that the contemplative life is the highest and most ex-
hausting of vocations, or not."[40] Just so, in later 1939, months and
months before, he had complained that the doctrincs of the the-
ologian MacMurray are distorted by his "determination to believe
in the existence of God," and had suggested that those doctrines
would lose little—would, really, gain a lot—if expressed as Auden
expressed them: "Man is aware that his actions do not express his
real nature. God is a term for what he imagines that nature to be.
Thus man is always making God in his own image."[41] (In a little
over a year he is sure that God is the Wholly Other.) Those years
were fun for Auden, but death for the theologians.[42]

After observing in Auden this permanent anxiety, guilt, and iso-
lation, adhered to with unchanging firmness in every stage of his
development, justified by different reasons in every stage, we can-
not fail to see that these "reasons" are reinforcing rationalizations
of the related attitudes which, not even rationally considered—
much less understood—have been for Auden a core impervious to
any change.

They form a core that Auden has scarcely attempted to change.
He is fond of the statement *Freedom is the recognition of necessity*, but he
does not seem to have recognized what it means in his own case:
that if he understands certain of his own attitudes as causally instead
of logically and ethically necessary—insofar as they are attitudes
produced by and special to his own training and culture—he can
free himself from them. But this Auden, like almost anyone, is par-
ticularly unwilling to understand. He is willing to devote all his en-
ergies and talents to finding the most novel, ingenious, or absurd ra-

tionalizations of the cluster of irrational attitudes he has inherited from a former self; the cluster, the self, he does not question, but instead projects upon the universe as part of the essential structure of that universe. If the attitudes are contradictory or logically absurd there, he saves them by taking Kierkegaard's position that everything really important is above logical necessity, is *necessarily* absurd. In the end he submits to the universe without a question; but it turns out that the universe is his own shadow on the wall beside his bed.

Let me make this plain with a quotation. At one time in his life Auden reviewed, in the New York *Times*, a new edition of *Grimm's Tales*; his moral and heartfelt sentences concluded:

> So let everyone read these stories till they know them backward and tell them to their children with embellishments—they are not sacred texts—and then, in a few years, the Society for the Scientific Diet, the Association of Positivist Parents, the League for the Promotion of Worthwhile Leisure, the Cooperative Camp for Prudent Progressives and all other bores and scoundrels can go jump in the lake.[43]

When would you guess that this sentence was written? Nineteen thirteen is the most likely date, I suppose: though at that time Auden was only six, we must remember that was an extremely precocious child; that fairy tales are sometimes given to children to review; and that the editor of the New York *Times* may very well have been acquainted with Auden's parents. Such a sentence plainly is written from the middle of an extremely *safe* world—a world that can be endangered by Cooperative Camps, saved by fairy tales; it is doubtful that anybody in Europe, since 1914, has ever felt as safe as this.

Actually the review was printed in 1944: within the months that held the mass-executions in the German camps, the fire-raids, Warsaw and Dresden and Manila; within the months that were preparing the bombs for Hiroshima and Nagasaki; within the last twelve months of the Second World War.

As logic Auden's advice is absurd: the S.S. Guards at Lublin and Birkenau had probably been told those stories a good deal more often than you or I or Auden. The secular world Auden dislikes has been produced by a thousand causes, among them these *Märchen* he idealizes and misunderstands; it could not be changed by one of the tiniest of the causes that have made it what it is. Of course, Auden hasn't made a contract with the world to be logical in perorations; the logical absurdity of the advice doesn't matter; but its moral and tactical absurdity does. In the year 1944 these prudent, progressive, scientific, cooperative "bores and scoundrels" were the enemies with whom Auden found it necessary to struggle. Were those your enemies, reader? They were not mine.

I don't want to sound pharisaical, so let me confess that most of them bored me quite as much as they did Auden. (Though they weren't scoundrels but *good*; a scoundrel or two would have been a welcome cloud.) But in an age of storks it seems foolish to complain first of King Log.

Lecture 6

Paid on Both Sides begins with a birth and ends with a death; begins with a woman sitting beside a child and a corpse and ends with a woman sitting beside a corpse. It begins with the account of the fight in which John Nower's father is killed and ends with the fight in which John Nower is killed. After we are told, first, of his father's death in the feud which is the permanent situation of the play, the mother talks about her sorrow, about memory, and about the vengeance her child will bring; and the chorus then speaks of the development of that or any child, of pressures and difficulties and moral demands of life. I will read the mother's speech and the speech of the chorus.

Not from this life, not from this life is any
To keep; sleep, day and play would not help there
Dangerous to new ghost; new ghost learns from many
Learns from old termers what death is, where.

Who's jealous of his latest company
From one day to the next final to us,

A changed one; would use sorrow to deny
Sorrow, to replace death; sorrow is sleeping thus.

Unforgetting is not to-day's forgetting
For yesterday, not bedrid scorning,
But a new begetting,
An unforgiving morning.

[*Baby squeals.*]

O see, he is impatient
To pass beyond this pretty lisping time:
There'll be some crying out when he's come there.

Chorus. Can speak of trouble, pressure on men
Born all the time, brought forward into light
For warm dark moan.
Though heart fears all heart cries for, rebuffs with mortal beat
Skyfall, the legs sucked under, adder's bite.
That prize held out of reach
Guides the unwilling tread,
The asking breath,
Till on attended bed
Or in untracked dishonour comes to each
His natural death.[1]

Immediately afterwards the grown John Nower, the hero of the play, is seen for the first time, in a scene with the comrade who is leaving the whole feud, emigrating to the colonies; as he is about to leave a spy interrupts them with news of a chance for a raid, a chance to kill the enemy leader who had killed John Nower's father. While they make their plans for their raid Auden gives to his audience a good many of the naturalistic details of the life of this specialized world of the play (mostly public-school details, here). While those left behind are waiting for news of the raid, they talk with uneasiness and dislike about the whole feud—it is a bitter accepted reality they have grown old with, cannot really imagine the world without.

T . . . Sometimes we read a sign, cloud in the sky,
The wet tracks of a hare, quicken the step
Promise the best day. But here no remedy
Is to be thought of, no news but the new death;
A Nower dragged out in the night, a Shaw
Ambushed behind the wall. Blood on the ground
Would welcome fighters. Last night at Hammergill
A boy was born fanged like a weasel. I am old,
Shall die before next winter, but more than once shall hear
The cry for help, the shooting round the house.

W. The best are gone.

Often the man, alone shut, shall consider
The killings in old winters, death of friends.
Sitting with stranger shall expect no good.

Spring came, urging to ships, a casting off,
But one would stay, vengeance not done; it seemed
Doubtful to them that they would meet again.

Fording in the cool of the day they rode
To meet at crossroads when the year was over:
Dead is Brody, such a man was Maul.

I will say this not falsely; I have seen
The just and the unjust die in the day,
All, willing or not, and some were willing.[2]

Anybody accustomed to sagas will give the same reminiscent
smile about some of this that he gives when, later in the play, a son
(unwillingly consenting to the murder his mother has persuaded
him to commit) finishes by saying, "Though I think that much will
come of this, chiefly harm." But here not only the surface, but the
skeleton, is that of the sagas; no modern work that I know has so
much the real feel of the sagas as certain parts of *Paid on Both Sides.*
John Nower and the other raiders come back and tell their story of
killing the enemy leader (they tell it in a theoretically absurd but

practically effective imitation of Anglo-Saxon verse); as they finish
a spy, the brother of that leader, is captured and brought in, and
John Nower (he never sounds so unsympathetic, so much a man of
action) orders him to be taken outside and shot. After this has been
done, Nower is left alone; in uneasy repugnance, he sees everything
that he does, everything that he is, as a false role, as wisdom—oth-
er people's wisdom—learned by rote; his official position, the ac-
tions he orders, the way he understands the world, all seem to him
so impossibly bad and senseless that he wants to go back past child-
hood, animalhood, into inanimate being.

> Always the following wind of history
> Of others' wisdom makes a buoyant air
> Till we come suddenly on pockets where
> Is nothing loud but us; where voices seem
> Abrupt, untrained, competing with no lie
> Our fathers shouted once. They taught us war,
> To scamper after darlings, to climb hills,
> To emigrate from weakness, find ourselves
> The easy conquerors of empty bays:
> But never told us this, left each to learn,
> Hear something of that soon-arriving day
> When to gave longer and delighted on
> A face or idea be impossible.
> Could I have been some simpleton that lived
> Before disaster sent his runners here;
> Younger than worms, worms have too much to bear.
> Yes, mineral were best: could I but see
> These woods, these fields of green, this lively world
> Sterile as moon.[3]

The chorus then makes a general paraphrase of, or variation upon,
his speech; it takes his situation as the typical human one—first it
regard[s] his troubles as the necessary difficulties of growth, but
then as that certain disaster to which all growth finally comes.

The Spring unsettles sleeping partnerships,
Foundries improve their casting process, shops
Open a further wing on credit till
The winter. In summer boys grow tall
With running races on the froth-wet sand,
War is declared there, here a treaty signed;
Here a scrum breaks up like a bomb, there troops
Deploy like birds. But proudest into traps
Have fallen. These gears which ran in oil for week
By week, needing no look, now will not work;
Those manors mortgaged twice to pay for love
Go to another.[4]

John Nower, alone in his chair, falls asleep; there then occur several characteristic episodes which are not on the same plane of reality as what has come before and after, but constitute a sort of nightmarish dream of Nower's, one in which all his guilts and doubts find expression. The spy (whom he has, in reality, already had executed) is the accused, and he himself the accuser, in a trial conducted by Santa Claus; John's own mother, equipped with an enormous baby-bottle, is the spy's guard. John himself makes a First World War patriotic speech about the Feud; enigmatic witnesses give troubling and ambiguous evidence, two of them in beautiful and haunting speeches.

B. In these days during the migrations, days
Freshening with rain reported from the mountains,
By loss of memory we are reborn,
For memory is death; by taking leave,
Parting in anger and glad to go
Where we are still unwelcome, and if we count
What dead the tides wash in, only to make
Notches for enemies. On northern ridges
Where flags fly, seen and lost, denying rumour
We baffle proof, speakers of a strange tongue.

. . . .

> *P.* Past victory is honour, to accept
> An island governorship, back to estates
> Explored as child; coming at last to love
> Lost publicly, found secretly again
> In private flats, admitted to a sign.
> An understanding sorrow knows no more,
> Sits waiting for the lamp, far from those hills
> Where rifts open unfenced, mark of a fall,
> And flakes fall softly softly burying
> Deeper and deeper down her loving son.[5]

Finally John, tortured by the accused man's groans, shoots him; a Doctor and his Boy enter and examine the body, in a mocking farcical scene that reads rather like the Knocking at the Gate scene in *Macbeth* rewritten by the Cocteau who wrote *Orphée*. Everything is beginning to change inside John's dream, nothing lasts for more than an instant, and the dream ends in a stranger and more personal form, as the accused and the accuser, reconciled now, plant a tree together, sharers of the same reality, of the queer natural compulsive bond that underlies their learned enmity.

> *John.* Sometime sharers of the same house
> We know not the builder nor the name of his son.
> Now cannot mean to them; boy's voice among dishonoured
>   portraits
> To dockside barmaid speaking
> Sorry through wires, pretended speech.
> *Spy.* Escaped
> Armies pursuit, rebellion and eclipse
> Together in a cart
> After all journeys
> We stay and are not known.
>
> Sharers of the same house
> Attendants on the same machine
> Rarely a word, in silence understood.[6]

(This last part of the dream, incidentally, has been the first intimation of the peace that John is going to conclude with the other side, of his coming marriage with the daughter of the enemy.) Then the lights come on and show John sitting in his chair alone, the dream over. Dick, the friend emigrating to the colonies, comes in and says goodbye to John, and by his existence reminds John of that other world outside the feud; afterwards John has a soliloquy which shows his guilt and dissatisfaction, and which ends in his determination to change everything, to reach somehow a natural warmth and steadiness and fertility, some sort of life beyond the institutionalized death of the feud.

> There is the city,
> Lighted and clean once, pleasure for builders
> And I
> Letting to cheaper tenants, have made a slum
> Houses at which the passer shakes his fist
> Remembering evil.
> Pride and indifference have shared with me, and I
> Have kissed them in the dark, for mind has dark,
> Shaded commemoration, midnight accidents
> In streets where heirs may dine.
>
> But love, sent east for peace
> From tunnels under those
> Bursts now to pass
> On trestles over meaner quarters
> A noise and flashing glass.[7]

He orders his horse, leaves; and the chorus then makes an extremely effective speech about what real change is like, its difficulties and laborious troubles, the new life in which it does finally wake up some morning.

> To throw away the key and walk away
> Not abrupt exile, the neighbours asking why,
> But following a line with left and right

An altered gradient at another rate
Learns more than maps upon the whitewashed wall
The hand put up to ask; and makes us well
Without confession of the ill.[8]

We now see developing on the stage—in fragmentary glimpses
of each side—some of that endless aimless fighting which is the old
everyday reality of this world. Suddenly the New appears: both
sides enter, a peace or armistice is made, and "the engagement is
announced of John Nower, eldest son of the late Mr. And Mrs.
George Nower of Lintzgfarth, Rookhope and Anne Shaw, only
daughter of the late Mr. and Mrs. Shaw of Nattrass, Garrigill." Af-
ter a few plausible, ambiguous, and uneasy remarks from each side,
only John and Anne are left on the stage; their love scene begins in
this way:[9]

J. On Cautly where a peregrine has nested, iced heather hurt the
knuckles. Fell on the ball near time, the forward stopped. Goodbye
now, he said, would open the swing doors. . . . These I remember,
but not love till now. We cannot tell where we shall find it, though
we all look for it till we do, and what others tell us is no use to us.

Some say that handsome raider still at large,
A terror to the Marshes, is truth in love;[10]

(The easy way in which the transition from prose to verse is man-
aged reminds one of the transition from *recitativo secco* to aria in a
Mozart opera—and *Paid on Both Sides* has an interesting relationship
to a kind of work in which ordinary speech, action, is in prose but
in *which what is lyric or thoughtful* or *conclusive, the "big" speeches*, are in
verse or are *sung*.)[11]

And we must listen for such messengers
To tell us daily 'To-day a saint came blessing
The huts.' 'Seen lately in the provinces
Reading behind a tree and people passing.'
But love returns;

At once all heads are turned this way, and love
Calls order—silenced the angry sons—
Steps forward, greets, repeats what he has heard
And seen, feature for feature, word for word.

Anne. Yes, I am glad this evening that we are together.
The silence is unused, death seems
    An axe's echo.

The summer quickens all,
Scatters its promises
To you and me no less
Though neither can compel.

J. The wish to last the year,
The longest look to live,
The urgent word survive
The movement of the air.

A. But loving now let none
Think of divided days
When we shall choose from ways,
All of them evil, one.

J. Look on with stricter brows
The sacked and burning town,
The ice-sheet moving down,
The fall of an old house.

A. John, I have a car waiting. There is time to join Dick before the
    boat sails. We sleep in beds where men have died howling.[12]

The ominous or uneasy insertions like *I have a car waiting* are making
sure that the conclusion of the play will not seem to anyone unex-
pected, and the chorus that ends the scene between John and Anne
is preparing us for the natural doom that waits for him, in spite of
his successful change.

The Spring will come,
Not hesitate for one employer who

Though a fine day and every pulley running
Would quick lie down; nor save the wanted one
That, wounded in escaping, swam the lake
Safe to the reeds, collapsed in shallow water.[13]

The ceremonies and random conversation of the Bridal Party are no more than a preparation for the scene between the Shaw mother and her son, a scene that begins with her fatal *John Nower is here* and ends with the son's promise to murder him. The son, Seth Shaw, is unwillingly persuaded by that Mother who stands for the Old Order of Things to do what will destroy the New (in the person of John Nower), will make everything continue as it has always been; it is precisely his weakness and clinging to his mother, his yearning to be thought strong, "a stern self-ruler," that not only overcome his unwillingness but that makes him end his soliloquy, "Of course I'll do it." He does; the briefly indicated murder and fighting offstage reestablish the old way of the world, so precariously and partially and temporarily escaped, and bring us to the conclusion of the play. The back curtains part and show us (just as, at the beginning of the play, we saw a woman beside a corpse) Anne sitting there with the corpse of John. She speaks with pure, grave, laconic bareness; her last line is a particular triumph of regret and concision:

Now we have seen the story to its end.
The hands that were to help will not be lifted,
And bad followed by worse leaves to us tears,
An empty bed, hope from less noble men.
I had seen joy
Received and given, upon both sides, for years.
Now not.[14]

And as the chorus ends the play with a kind of imitation of a Greek chorus that, for once, is far more than an imitation; the play ends with firmness, elevation, and generality—ends by accepting the necessity of what we have seen, and by admitting the possibility of something beyond it, of what we have not seen.

Though he believe it, no man is strong.
He thinks to be called the fortunate,
To bring home a wife, to live long.

But he is defeated; let the son
Sell the farm lest the mountain fall:
His mother and her mother won.

His fields are used up where the moles visit,
The contours worn flat; if there show
Passage for water he will miss it:

Give up his breath, his woman, his team;
No life to touch, though later there be
Big fruit, eagles about the stream.[15]

Paid on Both Sides is a quite serious play or saga (superficially mas-
querading as a charade) about a feud between two undifferentiated
tribal groups, half public-schools, half country families—rather
primitive Victorian industrial families. This feud, a permanent situa-
tion, is a sort of extended metaphor for ordinary life; the hero is born
into the feud, succeeds in it, grows out of it, tries to end it, and is fi-
nally destroyed by it. He is destroyed by necessity, the way of
things, not by any "tragic flaw" in himself; the moral view of the play
is serious and practical, not sermon-y and theoretical. The Necessi-
ty of the play is a necessity that, practically speaking, for the move-
ment of the play, is inescapable, but that finally and theoretically, is
not. The moral demands made upon the hero are opposed to the
more primitive and senseless demands of his society—he can meet
those demands only by changing a part of the society; he is tem-
porarily successful, but is destroyed when his world regresses from
this change. Morally he is successful, *does* really change himself;
there is a real catharsis at the end of the play. The play has a Greek
chorus which, at the end, does actually sound Greek for a moment;
usually it sounds saga-ish or Shakespearean. *Paid on Both Sides* is about
as Shakespearean as *Wozzeck*, and both its chorus and principal char-
acters are continually rising to soliloquies about human behavior and

existence which are both dramatic and essentially Shakespearean (But they are about as far from the ordinary imitation-Shakespeare purple passages as anything could be.)—the play seems to exist *in order that* these passages may occur. I realize that this *in order that* is an impeachment of the play, if we're comparing it with *Oedipus* or *Lear;* but comparing it with the verse dramas of our century, we can reply as the man accused of being a Southerner replied, "Suh, I admit the soft impeachment." How wonderful to have a verse play that exists *in order that* anything may occur; we're so used to verse plays that exist simply in order to be verse plays.

There is almost no Christian or Marxist influence on *Paid on Both Sides;* it is fairly psychoanalytical at bottom, as the hearer will have noticed—especially, I hope, the hearer of last week's lecture.[16] The most important influence on the play is the influence of the sagas— the more familiar you are with sagas the more you notice this. That Auden in one of the sagas—there are several Audens in them, it's a common Icelandic name, but I mean the Auden who owned a polar bear and took him to Constantinople, profitably exhibiting him to most of the rulers on the way—that Auden would have enjoyed *Paid on Both Sides* a great deal more, and a great deal more easily, than he would have enjoyed *The Cocktail Party* or *The Witch Is Not for Burning.*[17] It is, for one thing, the most concise play ever written—it is very short, hardly even a one-act play, but it has a sweep and range and scope, an imaginative grasp and depth, that the long verse plays of our time do not have.

The charade-convention of *Paid on Both Sides* apparently enabled Auden not to be self-conscious about writing dramatic verse, and thus helped to make it possible for him to write the wonderful dramatic-lyric verse that he often does write in the play. (Unfortunately, it is this charade-convention that makes readers reluctant to take the play seriously, to feel the verse for what it is.) Our time has had two main solutions to his problem of being self-conscious about writing a play in verse. One is that of Eliot in *The Cocktail Party*— where the baby, illegitimate as it is, is such a *little* baby, hardly verse at all. Eliot's explanation of his scansion is one of the funniest pieces of exposition ever written; I hate to spoil it by parody, but you feel, when you finish reading it, that you have been told that this is a verse with, ordinarily, one, two, three, or four stresses to a line, some of which, usually, come before, and some, usually, after, the caesura.[18] But even this is better than Christopher Fry's, whose very scansion manages to sound insincere.[19] I truly don't understand how even the rhythm of his lines can give that wonderful effect of pretentious, rhetorical, inconsequential virtuosity, of always just fooling around, of never even concernedly *meaning business*: every line is apologetically boasting that of course we must never forget that this is only verse, only play, not to be taken seriously for a moment—if it were *serious*, why then of course it would be prose. There is none of this in *Paid on Both Sides*, which is, at its best, probably the best verse Auden ever wrote, better than that of the poems he was writing at the time. Most of it is in that exhausted medium that Eliot loves to warn English dramatic poets against (and wrote in himself, so well and so dramatically, in "Gerontion")—I mean, of course, blank verse; but in Auden you are overjoyed by so much life and firmness and strength, at the queer naturalness of what often *ought* not to be natural at all—and it's only later you realize, "Why, it's blank verse."[20]

The trivial or absurd or unserious things are there on the surface, there to bother anybody, in *Paid on Both Sides*; underneath it is thoroughly serious, comes out of all the necessities of Auden's being, is without any real cheekiness, sure-fire effectiveness, posing, cant—it is a genuinely original play. (Though play does not seem exactly the right word for it, just as it does not seem exactly the right word for Yeats's *Plays for Dancers*; in *Paid on Both Sides*, even more than in them, the final interest has shifted from the action to the Shakespearean arias (of principals or chorus) to which the action leads up, in which the action is at once sublimated and embodied. These big speeches have as their great-grand fathers or great-grand mothers speeches like *Tomorrow and tomorrow and tomorrow; Time hath, my lord, a wallet at his back;* the Duke's speech in *Measure for Measure*, or any of a hundred more.[21] How live and changing and essentially dramatic such speeches are in Auden: they *are* morals in action, the concrete embodied development of some real being.[)]

Since all the addresses and difficulties of *Paid on Both Sides* are right out in public, not concealed under anything, this makes it extraordinarily easy for its readers to reject it as "queer; not really serious; awfully good *poetry* in it, but of course the whole thing's simply a charade—very young and experimental." The traditionalness of *Paid on Both Sides*, its true likeness to other plays, is far under the surface, a skeleton; modern verse plays usually wear their skeleton outside, like a lobster, and inside are hollow or soft or abnormal. All this surface similarly makes *Paid on Both Sides* so easy to reject that Auden himself, deluded wretch, has rejected it; or, rather, he hasn't *rejected* it, it doesn't even seem to him possible, any more, that *Paid on Both Sides* might be a successful work of art—flawed, but successful; he has hacked it to pieces, put six or seven speeches or choruses from it into his *Collected Poems*, and that's the end of *Paid on Both Sides!* Except in England—there the publisher made him print it, without a word changed, in his *Collected Shorter Poems.* I don't know how it can count as a *Collected Shorter Poem*, but God bless those publishers just the same! I don't know whether Auden needs to be saved from himself, but *Paid on Both Sides* certainly needs to be saved from him; we might start an early Auden society to be called The Friends of *Paid on Both Sides*, and give a performance of it every five years, in Iceland.

I've read the play many times, from 1932 to now, in army barracks and to school-girls, and its faults have come to seem to me, more and more, obvious and superficial faults: its virtues have come to seem to me a strength and reality and inevitability that can't be seen through, worn out, no matter how hard I look at it or how much I read it. Of course I can't *prove* any of this any more than I (or you or anybody else) can prove any judgment of taste. Nor can I make what I say thoroughly convincing, notably plausible, so that you can listen to what I say, read the play over once or twice, and rationally agree. The quality of a really unusual and original work of art is something you have to get by repeated rereadings, by real familiarity, just as you can only become really acquainted with an unusual and original piece of music by repeated rehearings, and not even that is enough—you also have to be a good reader. Someone said at one of our lectures early this fall: "Anybody can *read* poems;

the difficult thing is to make discursive statements about them, statements that you can discuss rationally." She and I have been living in different worlds. Anybody *can* make discursive statements about poems—half the people I know start making discursive statements a block and a half before they reach the poems. But to read the poems, really to read them—that *is* difficult. We are judging the poems, all right, but the poems are also judging us—and I hope my hearers will give *Paid on Both Sides* plenty of time to judge them, and not give it a chance to say, "Yeah, the usual sort of readers . . . Next!"

Auden has, from the beginning of his career, quite consistently written long works of one kind or another; during most of the 1940s he was writing very little else. The only one of these that seems to me really successful as a work of art is *Paid on Both Sides*, which I have already talked about at great length. The next, *The Orators*, Auden himself considers a failure—he says so in the preface to his *Collected Poems*—and it is no longer much read.[22] It seems disorganized, eccentric, and manneredly spasmodic to the average reader today; yet there are several good poems in it and, here and there, some decidedly effective "poetic prose." The *Address for a Prize Day* with which the book begins is a fairly good example—and the first example—of a genre in which Auden has specialized: a virtuoso, unqualifiedly brilliant, mockingly extravagant parody of some exaggerated sort of prose address made by a minister, a headmaster, Henry James, etc. I imagine that Auden first decided to write such passages after reading Joyce. There is no sort of writing which seems more congenial to Auden—it doesn't require any of the qualities in which he is lacking, and it does require all those which he has in abundance; he has always seemed to be cheered and buoyed up by having something to parody, even if its only his own style. Later this evening, when I come to his James parody in "The Sea and the Mirror," I will read paragraphs from it, from the sermon in *The Dog Beneath the Skin*, and from this Prize Day Address in *The Orators*, in order to show how good at this sort of thing he was to begin with, and how decidedly he improved: he can beat anybody alive at it.

This *Prize Day Address* is followed by a decidedly "modernist," cryptic, oddly organized, often brilliantly concrete and poetic series of recollections of a dead Leader, a real *Uncle*, written by a nostalgic, grieving, and guilty disciple. These recollections are followed by several pages of Lists, a sort of English public school imitation of the lists of Perse; one is startled to see those without their usual Asiatic trappings, their usual feeling of having been written by Salammbo just after she first read *Leaves of Grass*.[23] These lists end with an odd neo-primitive passage that seems to me a reasonably faithful imitation of Gertrude Stein; this may seem improbable, but judge for yourself:

> An old one is beginning to be two new ones. Two new ones are beginning to be two old ones. Two old ones are beginning to be one new one. A new one is beginning to be an old one. Something that has been done, that something is done again by someone. Nothing is being done but something being done again by someone.[24]

The next section, *Letter to a Wound*, is unadulterated Auden. It is a letter by a neurotic to his neurosis, by one of the perverse to his gradually grown into, accepted, cuddlingly relished perversion; it is all done in three pages, with economy, inevitability, and a queer fatal ease. Still, one moves with expectancy from these brief or fragmentary sections to a long one, the *Journal of an Airman*. It's the only diary I ever saw which includes a Mendelian inheritance chart, a sestina—quite an attractive one, too—some figures from the chapter on perception in a textbook of Gestalt psychology, and a series of Anglo-Saxon rhymes (about airplanes) which illustrate the letters of the alphabet from A to Z. But it has other virtues. The man who writes the diary is a kind of dream-condensation of the earlier figures of the disciple and the man who wrote the letter to the wound; he is a flyer too, planning a surreptitious revolt of his kind against the Enemy, those non-airmen with whose qualities hearers of these lectures are all too familiar; and he is, most important of all, a kleptomaniac—this obscurely-alluded-to kleptomania of his is a sort of symbolic symptom for all that is wrong with him, just as the Uncle he remembers worshipfully, the dead Leader, is a symbol of what is right.[25] The diary goes on, getting closer and closer to the day of the final surrealistically described fantasy-revolt that is going to put an end to Things As They Are; but, just before it, the Airman realizes the meaning of what, in a dream a few nights before, his uncle had said to him; he realizes that (to quote Auden)

1. The power of the enemy is a function of our resistance, therefore
2. The only efficient way to destroy it [is] self-destruction, the sacrifice of all resistance, reducing him to the state of a man trying to walk on a frictionless surface.
3. Conquest can only proceed by absorption of, i.e. infection by, the conquered. The true significance of my hands. 'Do not imagine that you, no more than any other conqueror, escape the mark of grossness.' They stole to force a hearing.[26]

This is the first occurrence, in Auden's work, of this idea: an idea that was to be important to him in a few years. The Airman, in the next two days, settles his affairs and writes to E, the girl he is in love with: "O understand, darling. God just loves us all, but means to be obeyed; and unaffecting is our solid tear"; he then prepares to go up and commit suicide: the journal ends with the calm, prosaic, triumphant "mean temperature, 34° F. Fair. Some cumulus cloud at 10,000 feet. Wind easterly and moderate. Hands in perfect order."[27]

The rest of *The Orators* consists of six "Odes"; the long, well known "To My Pupils" (it is called in the *Collected Poems* "Which Side Am I Supposed to Be On?" and is included in Untermeyer's anthology) is one of Auden's better poems, the largest and most impressive of his early poems about the imaginary war which he was so fond of. Another, the third ode—it begins *What siren zooming is sounding our coming*, and is dedicated to that Edward Upward who is the hero of Isherwood's *Lions and Shadows*—is a direct, frightening, and effective poem, though no one reads it much, and it's not included in the *Collected Poems*; the sixth ode, the one that begins *Not, Father, further do prolong / Our necessary defeat*, is a felt and serious poem that few poets would have the right to be ashamed of.[28] As for the other three odes, the best you can say for them is that one is the only English imitation of Vachel Lindsay's "Bryan, Bryan, Bryan." But three successes out of six tries is, of course, an extraordinarily high proportion for any poet who ever lived; and Auden follows them with a little lyric (called *Epilogue*) which, like the *Prologue*, has charms of its own. No, *The Orators* is still decidedly worth reading, even though it is eccentric, sometimes absurd, and fashionably and appallingly disorganized. And, also, it has by now all the charm of a period piece, and many of the worst things in it are as delightful as some eighteenth-century ode beginning, *Inoculation, heavenly Maid!*

About four years later Auden wrote the first of his long poems; it is, and was intended to be, inconsequential light verse. In this *Letter to Lord Byron* Auden deliberately writes in the style of the most mocking, casual, and carelessly written parts of *Don Juan*—the poem is full of fun and "information of interest to the biographer." (Auden's sonnet sequence inspired by the war in China I will consider along with the other long piece it most resembles, *The Quest*, though it was written before the next poem I'll consider.) This, *New Year Letter*, consists of a couple of thousand tetrameter couplets about— well, it's always hard to say what long didactic expository poems are about, but one feels quite safe in saying the *New Year Letter* is about the Modern World and how it got to be Modern, about Auden— the poet—and his relations to Things in General.[29] It is what people always call a "real *tour de force*"; and it is, on a rather low level, in a rather easy way, a real success. (It is never quite as pleasant to read as it was the first time one read it.) It is an odd compound of the *Essay on Man* and the *Epistle to Dr. Arbuthnot*, done in a very run-on version of Swift's most colloquial couplets. Pope would be bewildered at the ideas, and make fun of (or, once or twice, patronizingly commend) the versification; but he would relish the Wit, Learning, and Sentiment—the last becoming, as it so often does, plural and Improving; and the Comprehending Generality, Love of Science, and Social Benevolence might warm him into the murmur, "Well enough for such an age."

New Year Letter contains Auden's ideas about almost everything (Life and the Good Life, Art and Society, Politics, Morals, Love, the Devil, the Decline of the West, Economic Man). Auden's earlier

ideas had had an arbitrary *effective* quality, a "personality" value, al-
most like ideas in D.H. Lawrence or Pound. The ideas in *New Year
Letter* are on a considerably higher level—and no wonder: Auden has
got most of them from some extremely brilliant sources: the bibli-
ography at the end of the poem is not in the least a joke, and you
can find specific sources (in Kierkegaard, Kafka, Köhler, Colling-
wood, Niebuhr, Nietzsche, Freud, and all the rest) for the great ma-
jority of the ideas in *New Year Letter*—but the combination of them,
the specialization or extension of them, is entirely Auden's. Most of
the important ideas, the ones that serve as a framework, come from
one particular tradition in the thought of the last hundred years or
so; but the lesser ideas, the decorations of the Christmas tree, come
from almost everywhere—the range of Auden's interests and infor-
mation is quite astonishing, and the reader often exclaims with a
laugh, "What a queer thing for a *poet* to know!" The poem sometimes
seems written by our old eighteenth-century friend, the Citizen of
the World, who finds French, German, Latin, Greek, and Italian
quite naturally and rather often upon his lips, especially in witty or
ecstatically lyric passages.

The poem is thoroughly and rapidly readable; Auden handles
with easy virtuosity humorous and serious material—sometimes his
method of joining them verges on simple Byronic alternation, but
they tend to be swept together by the tone and verse-movement,
rapid, informal, and easily adaptable.

The thought of the poem is, often, a little rapid and superficial,
but the movement of the verse is, always, just a little more of both,
so that you feel it would be absurd to object: after all, when you're
being swept down rapids in a canoe, à la *Hudibras*, it seems a little
priggish to shout above the roar: "The *Critique of Judgment* goes into
all this *much* more systematically."[30] The poetry, strained through so
many abstractions, diluted by so many transitions and Necessities of
Composition, often *does* get thin, often does make the reader think,
"These are run-on couplets in every sense of the word"; but Auden
has accomplished the entirely unexpected[,] an (in our time) im-
probable feat of making a readable and moderately successful long
poem—or, by the severest standards, an interesting piece of verse—

out of an intelligent and comprehensive discussion. The poem is kept arresting and concrete by many devices: wit, rhetoric, all sorts of unexpected images (drawn from the sciences, often); surprising quotations, allusions, technical terms, points of view, shifts of tone; Auden treats ideas in terms of their famous advocates, expresses situations in arresting analogous conceits; and he specializes in unexpected coordinates, the exquisitely ridiculous or incongruous term. But the poem, alas, is never the slightest real competition for Pope—it lacks the necessary immediacy and finality of presentation, it is at a remove; the urgency and reality have been diluted. Evil is talked about a great deal, hardly once brought home to the reader; the devil, talk as he will, is only a knowing teddy bear—there is about the whole poem a faint sweet smell of *to understand everything is to forgive everything*, and we feel that the poem, and everything else, is going to be All Right in the End. When one remembers Auden's early poetry at his best, one feels unreasonably—no, reasonably—homesick for the fleshpots of Egypt, and grumbles "This *is* the wilderness."

In the notes to the poem there are quotations, aphorisms, exposition, anecdotes, verse, even a poem or two: if not God's plenty, at least, plenty. A few notes are valuable in themselves, some explain or amplify or locate the poem's ideas; but these water a positive desert of Good Sense: machine-made parables, logic-chopping paradoxes, humorlessly exaggerated half-truths, with which we wearily dissent or impatiently agree. The notes specialize in neither the High nor the Low, but the Mean Sublime. To the question "What is the only thing that always remains work, that can never give us aesthetic satisfaction," Auden gives Kierkegaard's answer, "*The moral*"; the victims of Auden's insistent raids on The Moral can ruefully agree.[31]

Auden's next longish piece, a sonnet sequence called *The Quest*, is one of the most mannered and mechanical things he has ever written: as soon as you know the subject of the poems (the fairy-tale quest, with all the specialized symbolic significance that Auden is accustomed to give it) and their manner (they are rationalized Rilke sonnets—I am using *rationalized* primarily in its industrial sense)—as

soon as you know these two things you know all too well what one
of the sonnets is going to be like; or, if you don't, you do know as
soon as you have read the first couple of poems. The manner, the
rhythm, the rhymes very soon get to seem to the reader an oiled,
oblivious little machine of abstract and habitual fancy into which
anything about quests can be inserted and, in fifteen seconds, be
processed, to emerge as a drily shining sonnet; the reader feels,
"Can anything so typical be true? If poems are so much alike as this,
why not read one and be done with it?" This isn't fair, of course—
there *are* good lines, ingenious or acute ideas; but the reader in his
drugged monotony, is in no shape to be fair—it is like asking a man
to be fair to newsreels, and to admit that one newsreel *is* different
from another. Auden says, about the Way to Salvation, in the most
attractive and truthful couplet in these sonnets, "And how reliable
can any truth be that is got / By observing oneself and then just in-
serting a Not?"[32] Well, how good can any poem be that is got / by
observing one's poetry and then not inserting a Not? The epigraph
of this sonnet sequence ought to be; "You know my methods, Wat-
son." Let me read you a typical one, "The Adventurers."[33]

Spinning upon their central thirst like tops,
They went the Negative Way towards the Dry;
By empty caves beneath an empty sky
They emptied out their memories like slops

Which made a foul marsh as they dried to death,
Where monsters bred who forced them to forget
The lovelies their consent avoided; yet,
Still praising the Absurd with their last breath,

They seeded out into their miracles:
The images of each grotesque temptation
Became some painter's happiest inspiration;

And barren wives and burning virgins came
To drink the pure cold water of their wells,
And wish for beaux and children in their name.

Most of what I have said about *The Quest* applies to the sonnet sequence *In Time of War*; Auden even, very honestly and with appealing naturalness, makes half of one sonnet a tribute to Rilke, so that only those completely unacquainted with Rilke's poetry will be able to overlook its part in these poems of Auden's.[34] But an occasional line in these poems has more reality than anything in *The Quest*, and an occasional sonnet has a political, oratorical, dismayingly sentimental rhetoric, worse than anything in *The Quest*; the long verse commentary applies the methods of "Spain 1937" to the history of mankind, and smothers under the blanket of the Official Address, of the Institutional Auden, both some beautiful phrases and some interesting ideas.

"For the Time Being," Auden's "Christmas Oratorio," is one of the best-written, most doctrinaire, and most thoroughly characteristic of all Auden's long pieces; it is a work of arresting and efficient virtuosity. Auden seems so pleased at getting to do all he likes best, and to say all that he has come to believe most, that some of the most serious passages have an astonishing bounce and lift; I think he should have used *Heigh ho, heigh ho, it's off to work we go* (sung in the Seven Dwarfs' cheerfulest tones) as an epigraph for the piece.[35]

Auden calls "The Sea and the Mirror" a "Commentary on Shakespeare's *The Tempest*"; it reminds me of some piece like Liszt's fantasia on themes from Don Giovanni—perhaps *a free fantasia on themes from "The Tempest"* would be an accurate subtitle for it. Auden's work is one long conceit, an extended metaphor the terms of which he has derived from *The Tempest*: what the metaphor stands for, the main subject of the work, is the Morality of Art—or, rather, the question Is Art Immoral? Auden's answer, up until the last couple of paragraphs, is nothing to make Plato and Tolstoy turn over in their graves, except perhaps with delight; but the final rescuing paragraphs are certainly enough to make Goethe and Arnold turn over in *theirs*. I can't think of any attack on works of art which is as much of a work of art as Caliban's address to the audience; it is a very complicated, sophisticated, rhetorically effective, cunningly condemnatory analysis of both the production and consumption of works of art—Auden has used, to make his argument more plausible and more aesthetically satisfying, every device that wide reading and long writing can suggest. Even the style is rocket-assisted James: the reader murmurs, his eyes widening: "Who would have thought the old man had so much blood in him?"[36] But, reluctant as I am to leave it for even a moment, I had better talk first about the earlier portions of "The Sea and the Mirror."

The work begins with a little preface in which the Stage Manager addresses the critics: the second and fourth stanzas are particularly attractive, and in the fourth Auden manages to combine *The rest is silence* and *Ripeness is all* into a quiet, conversational, and—unexpectedly—a fairly satisfactory conclusion to the poem. Part 1 of "The Sea and the Mirror" is a long speech which Prospero, the old writer, makes to Ariel, his gift: into the speech are inserted, somewhat arbitrarily, two mocking and rather blatant ballads, more then vaguely reminiscent of some of Yeats's—the delicate lyric which concludes the section seems more properly there, a quite successful ending. But Auden is not altogether successful in getting Prospero's speech to sound like an old man's—Prospero's legs have too springy and Audenesque a stride; some of the poems in which the poet himself speaks, written five or six years later, actually do sound far more like an old man speaking, and one wishes that Auden could have written this particular section of "The Sea and the Mirror" at that time instead. *What* Prospero says about Art is particularly interesting, and there is enough truth in it to disquiet anyone, though not enough to convince everyone. He says that magic, art, is "the power to enchant / That comes through disillusion"; the artist, by not acting, by sitting still and letting his gift, Ariel, do everything for him, can give the artist knowledge he couldn't otherwise have, redeem and make acceptable the sorrows and vices and weaknesses that would be unbearable otherwise, make, in the work of art, "all that we are not / stare back at what we are."[37] But all Ariel's tricks were really a test to find the weakness through which he could corrupt Prospero, and Prospero, who had made two promises ("to hate nothing and to ask nothing for its love"), broke them both—his hatred made him tempt Antonio into treason and his "wish / For absolute devotion" made him ruin Caliban, made Caliban Prospero's "impervious disgrace."[38] Of the metaphorical meanings here, one is clear and the other is not: Caliban stands, one learns later, for the life which the artist leaves undeveloped, as opposed to the talents he develops; but what Antonio stands for, or his tempting into Treason, I don't see, so far as the artist his life, and his gifts are concerned.[39]

Prospero has finally broken free from his unreal life with Ariel to the real life of religious awareness: he says that he feels as if he had been on a drunk all his life, and were now cold sober "with all my unanswered wishes and unwashed days / Stacked up around my life."[40] He now feels as if all he had easily pretended to do in art he now has actually to do, with difficulty, in life. When, back in Italy, the servants settle him in a chair with rugs over him, he alone will know that he is really "sailing alone, out over seventy thousand fathoms"; but will he be able to resist telling the servants, and as he does, be punished by sinking into that abyss?[41] (*Sailing alone over seventy thousand fathoms* is Kierkegaard's phrase for the life of dread, *angst*, religious consciousness, and Auden has borrowed it for Prospero.)[42] Prospero goes on to confess that art has taught him neither to act nor to know: he says,

> Can I learn to suffer
>   Without saying something ironic or funny
> On suffering? I never suspected the way of truth
>   Was a way of silence where affectionate chat
> Is a robber's ambush and even good music
>   In shocking taste; and you, of course, never told me.
> If I peg away at it honestly every moment,
>   And have luck, perhaps by the time death pounces
> His stumping question, I shall just be getting to know
>   The difference between moonshine and daylight. . . .[43]

Neither the argument nor the poem seem to me altogether successful—the poem is a little too weak, the argument a lot too strong—but both are carefully, thoughtfully, and manneredly but unpretentiously worked out; they prepare beautifully for the full-scale attack on the subject that Auden is saving for Caliban's speech.

Part 2 consists of a speech from each of the more important char-
acters in *The Tempest* (except for Ariel, who delivers the postscript of
the work). These speeches vary remarkably, both in form, in con-
tent, and in merit; they range from a good sestina to a bad couplet,
and each is followed by Antonio's mordant and superior contradic-
tion of what has just been said (Antonio represents roughly the will
to deny, Original Sin, that which, as Auden phrases it—"by choice
myself alone"—will never give in to Prospero: he represents the
proud hard separate element in people which it is impossible to
change into love in real life, and which therefore makes it necessary
for Prospero to remain an artist, a magician—the fragments of the
broken wand rejoin themselves, the burnt books reappear, anything
Prospero wears is a magic robe as long as Antonio can, by his deny-
ing separateness, force Prospero to remain the magician, the
"melancholy mentor, the grown-up man, the adult in his pride."[44]

Ferdinand's speech, a very lyric, rapturous, ecstatic one, is man-
neredly unconvincing, and has a peculiarly sentimental last line,
most of it borrowed from James [every word in the line begins with
a capital letter]: "The Right Required Time, The Real Right Place, O
Light."[45] Stephano's ballade is a great deal more attractive than this,
just as it is more attractive than Adrian and Francisco's couplet,
which sounds (as Auden meant it to) quite as if it were being recit-
ed by Beverly Nichols and Cecil Beaton: "Good little sunbeams
must learn to fly, / But it's madly ungay when the goldfish die."[46]
Sebastian's sestina is a quiet, complicated, thoughtful, sincere-
sounding sestina about the blessings of Exposure, of Failure, of ad-
mitting to ourselves what even the world at last knows about us,
that we are what we are. Sebastian begins

> My rioters all disappear, my dream
> Where Prudence flirted with a naked sword,
> Securely vicious, crumbles; it is day;
> Nothing has happened; we are all alive,
> I am Sebastian, wicked still.

And ends by saying "I smile because I tremble, glad today / To be
ashamed, not anxious, not a dream."[47] He has been pushed from the

anxious, lying prison of his dreams out into the humiliating, reas-
suring daylight of reality. It is one of the best of these poems, as is
Alonso's speech to his son, a series of stanzas each of which locates
(a little too methodically, sometimes) the ruler, any ruler, on the
narrow human razor's edge between the sea and the desert—Auden
uses for both sea and desert some of the surrealist, Breughelish im-
ages which he was to learn to use so very effectively during the late
1940s. Trinculo, the clown, has a little poem, quite magical and
touching in parts, about the unlucky clown; it begins

> Mechanic, merchant, king,
> Are warmed by the cold clown
> Whose head is in the clouds
> And never can get down.
>
> Into a solitude
> Undreamed of by their fat
> Quick dreams have lifted me;
> The north wind steals my hat,
>
> On clear days I can see
> Green acres far below,
> And the red roof where I
> Was Little Trinculo.[48]

Miranda finishes Part 2 with a more conventionally magical, but
quite attractive, villanelle; we then come to Caliban's long prose
speech. Its style is an extremely witty, exaggerated and mocking
adaptation of Henry James's later style, galvanized into a newer
and stranger life by tremendous, characteristically Audenish injec-
tions of incongruity and poetic concreteness. The style has been
rather notably difficult for readers and reviewers—so much so that
one almost never sees any discussion of *what* it says, but only dis-
cussions of how it says it. I have made a sort of highly concen-
trated paraphrase of its argument; I will read this, to indicate as
well as I can what it is about, and will then read one of the last
pages of the speech to show what the style is capable of in Auden's

daemonic hands—there are passages as inimitable as anything well can be.[49]

"Real life is best described figuratively, as the most atrocious production[,] by the most provincial opera company, of the grandest grand opera: we have not done one single thing right, we realize at last; and we realize that—just as always before—we hang hopeless over the abyss, our Reason absurd, our will surrendered. It is then that we hear, no longer our voice['s] distortion, but the real Word, our only reason for being; and we see that it is not in spite of but *through* our faults and vices that the Other Life blesses us, in the reversed terms of the mirror-image. The gulf between real life and the stage is a representative sign of that between the secular and the Wholly Other Life, the religious life. One is the mirror image of the other—we positively envisage Mercy in its negative image of Judgment; and our ruined mess represents the 'righteous obligation,' the 'molar pardon' of the perfected Whole that extends to us, still, its 'grand old prospect of wonder and width,' its 'restored relation.'"[50]

What Auden *says* in the poem is far more than our/my seriously elaborated half-truth; but I think the speech, so far as its argument is concerned, is more of an aesthetic success than a success in aesthetics. It sometimes is a dazzling aesthetic success, the baroque of our days; let me finish with its wonderful description of The World of Childhood:

Carry me back, Master, to the cathedral town where the canons run through the water meadows with butterfly nets and the old women keep sweetshops in the cobbled side streets, or back to the upland mill town (gunpowder and plush) with its grope-movie and its poolroom lit by gas, carry me back to the days before my wife had put on weight, back to the years when beer was cheap and the rivers really froze in winter . . . Give me my passage home, let me see that harbour once again just as it was before I learned the bad words. Patriarchs wiser than Abraham mended their nets on the modest wharf; white and wonderful beings undressed on the sand dunes; sunset glittered on the plate-glass windows of the Marine Biological Station; far off on the extreme horizon a whale spouted. Look, Uncle, look. They have broken my glasses and I have lost my silver whistle. Pick me up, Uncle, let little Johnny ride away on your massive shoulders to recover his green kingdom, where the steam rollers are as friendly as the farm dogs and it would never become necessary to look over one's left shoulder or clench one's right first in one's pocket.[51]

Audience, your questions.[52] Your complaints show that you have escaped from the spell of the world of childhood, where everything was theatrically magical, and you its magician; you are now in the actual world, on the wrong side of the mirror, and understand the irreconcilable difference between Caliban's reiterated categorical actuality and Ariel's varied hypothetical propositions. (I didn't, here, neglect to paraphrase the transition—there was none.)[53] Life is a railway journey. But only a few moments are spent travelling, all the others are spent in stations, depots, sidings. Here, now you are at Grand Central—all the ways go out everywhere from here: *stay here*—you'll never be better off than here in your potentiality; here Ariel and Caliban can warn you not to ask them to be your guides when you meet them outside when they can't refuse.

Most of you will ask Caliban, Cupid, to take you back *home*, to childhood, to the womb, away from the restrictions and deprivations and lim[it]ations of reason, back to free, meaningless, incoherent sensation. And Caliban will take you to the ultimately liberal condition: moonlight on the geysers and lava of a volcanic plateau, the only subject you, the only objects all undifferentiated, uncaring, meaningless, purely tautological repetition. And you will fall into the abyss of silence and despair "all fact your single drop, all value your pure alas."[54]

But you intellectuals will ask Ariel to deliver you from the insane, emotional, *human* chaos of all particulars, to the ideal, abstract, perfectly Platonic—even Parmenidean—One.[55] And he will deliver you to a world, *of pure volition, of complete possibility, of Mind, pure, autonomous, intolerable.*[56]

Notes

Introduction

1. Edward Mendelson, *Early Auden* (1981; Cambridge, Mass.: Harvard University Press, 1983), 107.
2. William Pritchard, *Randall Jarrell: A Literary Life* (New York: Farrar, Straus and Giroux, 1990), 91.
3. Randall Jarrell, *Complete Poems* (New York: Farrar, Straus and Giroux, 1969), 375.
4. Jarrell, *Complete Poems*, 427.
5. Jarrell, *Complete Poems*, 378.
6. Jarrell, *Complete Poems*, 381.
7. Jarrell, *Kipling, Auden, and Co.* (New York: Farrar, Straus and Giroux, 1980), 77, 83. Compare the remarks about modernism and romanticism in Mendelson, *Early Auden*, 22, 203.
8. Jarrell, *Kipling*, 45.
9. The most vigorous discussion of Jarrell's evolving debts to Auden is Ian Sansom, "'Flouting Papa': Randall Jarrell and W. H. Auden," in *In Solitude, for Company: W. H. Auden After 1940*, ed. Katherine Bucknell and Nicholas Jenkins, Auden Studies 3 (Oxford: Clarendon, 1995). On Audenesque elements in Jarrell's early poetry, see

also Pritchard, *Randall Jarrell*, 42–45, 60–62. Sansom and others, such as Michael Wood, find verbal echoes of Auden in later poems, culminating in Jarrell's "The Old and the New Masters," an unmistakable, strongly argued response to Auden's "Musée de Beaux Arts": see Sansom, " 'Flouting Papa,' " 282–87 and Wood, "Keeping the Reader Alive," *New York Review of Books*, 2 December, 1999.

10. Sansom, " 'Flouting Papa,' " 273–88.

11. Mary Jarrell, ed., *Randall Jarrell's Letters*, 2nd ed. (Charlottesville: University of Virginia Press, 2002), 3.

12. Jarrell, ed., *Letters*, 124, 128.

13. Jarrell, *The Third Book of Criticism* (New York: Farrar, Straus and Giroux, 1969), 149–50.

14. A preeminent advocate of Auden's later work writes that his "most ambitious poems in the earlier months of 1941 had expressed a guiltless religiosity in which evil was never chosen and for which the most suitable images were plaster saints and a faceless absolute. He later characterized this episode of his life and work in a single word: 'frivolity.' " Edward Mendelson, *Later Auden* (New York: Farrar, Straus and Giroux, 1999), 174.

15. Monroe Spears, ed., *Auden: A Collection of Critical Essays* (Englewood Cliffs, N.J.: Prentice-Hall, 1964), 3; John Haffenden, ed., *W. H. Auden: The Critical Heritage* (London: Routledge and Kegan Paul, 1983), 44.

16. Haffenden, ed., *W. H. Auden*, 91–92, 160–165.

17. James Southworth, *Sowing the Spring* (1940; reprint, Freeport, N.Y.: Books for Libraries, 1968), 135.

18. Quoted in Peter Firchow, *W. H. Auden: Contexts for Poetry* (Newark: University of Delaware Press, 2002), 194.

19. Jarrell, *Pictures from an Institution* (1954; reprint, Chicago: University of Chicago Press, 1986), 243.

20. Jarrell, ed., *Letters*, 216.

21. Randall Jarrell, *Poetry and the Age* (1953; reprint, Gainesville: University Press of Florida, 2001), xxi.

22. Princeton's student newspaper, the *Daily Princetonian*, for 1951 through 1952 makes no mention of them, but it does note public lectures by visiting faculty and readings by visiting writers, including Malcolm Cowley ("Modern Writing to Be Discussed by Novel Critics," 13 May 1952) and William Carlos Williams

("W. C. Williams, New Jersey Physician, to Speak Today," 19 March 1952).

23. Francis Fergusson, "Annual Report to the President of Princeton University on the Seminars in Literary Criticism for 1951–52," University archives, Mudd Library, Princeton University. Jarrell's letters reveal that he attended Read's lectures unenthusiastically, and the "lovely Dominican monk" Father de Menasce's with unfeigned interest; they make no mention of Castro (Jarrell, ed., *Letters*, 281, 287, 298).

24. Fergusson, "Annual Report."

25. Fergusson, "Annual Report."

26. R. P. Blackmur, "A Statement with Respect to the Creative Writing Section of the Creative Arts Program," 13 June 1957, Blackmur papers, Firestone Library, Princeton University. (When Blackmur went on leave for the fall of 1952, the *Daily Princetonian* for April 25 of that year reported that his duties as head of creative writing would fall to "Delmar Schultz.")

27. Stauffer died in the summer of 1952, before he could get home (*Daily Princetonian*, 22 September 1952).

28. Because Jarrell wrote letters over several days and then posted them all at once, and because the envelopes in the Berg Collection do not always match the papers that adjoin them in the MS folders, few dates on these letters can be more than approximate (the published *Letters* contain only some of the letters, and those). To compare the dates on envelopes attached to the letters with dates from official Princeton documents is to see the troubles with the former: a letter dated 12 May 1952 promises that RJ will "make my last lecture tomorrow"; "Just think! tomorrow the Auden lectures are over." Yet a letter dated 21 May exclaims, "How near the End of the Auden Lectures is getting. Glory, glory!"

29. Jarrell, *Complete Poems*, 477, 481.

30. Berg Collection. Randall copied for Mary "This lunar beauty," part of "Consider this and in our time," "Ours in untracked dishonour," and "Before this loved one"; the letter can be dated only by Jarrell's comment: "To think this is the last letter I'll write until the end of October!"

31. Berg Collection. For the published version, see *Letters* 325.

32. Berg Collection; the "last book" is *Nones* (1951).

33. Conversation with Mary Jarrell, 24 October 2003.
34. For Randall's description of those events, see Jarrell, ed., *Letters* 340–46.
35. The Princeton English Club files include an invitation to see "Mr. Randall Jarrell, reading from his own poems, Nassau Club Grill Room, Wed. May 14 at 8pm (60 cents for room and refreshment)" (Princeton University archives, Mudd Library).
36. Jarrell, ed., *Letters*, 339.
37. This letter—assuming the date on it accurate—establishes that the material on "The Sea and the Mirror" must have been delivered in lecture 4, 5, or 6; the quoted sentence survives in the folder the Berg Collection labels as lecture 6.
38. Jarrell, ed., *Letters*, 343–44. The letter describes an argument between Blackmur and Jarrell, which confirms that the lecture given on 25 April was the lecture that the Berg records (and that appears here) as lecture 3.
39. Berg Collection.
40. Jarrell, ed., *Letters*, 344, 347. For more on Kahler's, and Blackmur's, social circle at Princeton, see Eileen Simpson, *Poets in Their Youth* (New York: Farrar, Straus and Giroux, 1990), chapters four and nine.
41. Jarrell, ed., *Letters*, 347.
42. Berg Collection. The letter continues: "Whenever I grouse (and I do thousands and thousands of times) over these Auden lectures I cheer myself up by thinking that at least I can use them over again this summer at Indiana." Jarrell taught Auden's poetry at some length (as his letters to Mary reveal) at the School of Criticism in Bloomington, Indiana, during the summer of 1952; he may have redelivered some of the Princeton lectures as well.
43. Jarrell, *Kipling*, 226–230; Jarrell, ed., *Letters*, 424. Sometime in the early 1960s Jarrell denied Monroe Spears permission to reprint "Changes of Attitude and Rhetoric" in Spears's collection of critical essays on Auden (Spears, ed., *Auden*, 4). Jarrell may have wanted to save it for a critical book he was still planning, though he may also have turned against its conclusions: decisions he made during late 1963 and 1964 do not, in any case, necessarily say much about his earlier, more settled intentions (see Pritchard, *Randall Jarrell*, 290–93).
44. The "Auden notebook" also contains, for example, notes for Jar-

rell's review of *The Fall of the City* (published in 1943, possibly start-
ed years before); notes for his review of the poet Horace Grego-
ry (1941); and notes for "Freud to Paul." Jarrell used each of his
notebooks for several projects and tended to use several note-
books simultaneously, some of them for years at a stretch.

45. "That poem in *Harper's*" is almost certainly "Under Which Lyre"
    (*Harper's*, June 1947, 508–9), which fits Jarrell's description; "Pre-
    cious Five" (*Harper's*, October 1950, 58–59) also makes a good ex-
    ample of Auden's postwar "frivolity" (the poem begins "Be patient,
    solemn nose"), but it does not attack "boring moralists," as "Under
    Which Lyre" does.

46. This list suggests either that Jarrell planned to publish his writ-
    ing on *Nones* in the *Yale Review* after he had delivered it as a lec-
    ture or (more likely) that Jarrell was still making tables of con-
    tents for his book on Auden long after he had delivered the
    lectures, since his review of *The Shield of Achilles* (incorporating
    some of his comments on *Nones*) appeared in the *Yale Review* in
    1955; Jarrell wrote for the *Yale Review* only in 1955 and 56 (Jar-
    rell, *Kipling*, 221 ff.).

47. Berg Collection.

48. Berg Collection; Jarrell, ed., *Letters*, 287; compare Jarrell's 1955 de-
    scription of Auden's "lined, sagging, fretful, consciously powerful
    old lion's face" (Jarrell, *Kipling*, 228).

49. Berg Collection.

50. Simpson, *Poets in Their Youth*, 110.

51. Jarrell, *Poetry and the Age*, 90.

Lecture 1

*These notes attempt to attribute all quotations and references in Jarrell's MSS,
including several inexact quotations and paraphrases, whether from Auden or
from other sources. (Jarrell sometimes paraphrases from memory, but uses quote
marks anyway when he is quoting prose.) A few references we have been unable
to find. I also omit citations to very famous short phrases (e.g., Heraclitus' "one
never steps into the same river twice") for which Jarrell would not have needed
nor used a source. All the material originally written in French, Russian or Ger-
man which Jarrell quotes or cites existed in English translation by 1951; where
possible I give the English translation Jarrell would have used.*

The lecture consists of twenty-nine MS and five TS pages, which represent continuous but, on occasion, overlapping text (with no lacunae). The five TS pages duplicate the first eight pages of the MS; here, as with his other texts written for oral presentation (such as "Is American Literature American?"), Jarrell seems to have written the lecture in longhand, taken a longhand draft and begun to type it up, then given up typing halfway. Page numbers within the MS are consecutive except that it includes two pages numbered "5"; the first p. 5 is followed by pages numbered 5a, 5b, . . . 5d, after which the next page (which introduces a new paragraph and a new theme) is again numbered 5; 5d contains text on both sides. Page numbers within the TS are consecutive from 1 to 5 except that the last two TS pages duplicate each other and clearly represent successive drafts (see note 4 below); the complete MS lecture is either intermediate between the two TS versions, or later than the later of the two TSS. The first MS page contains the title "The Best of Auden," probably not in RJ's handwriting. This text represents the latest available version of each piece of the lecture, using TS in preference to MS except as noted; I do not indicate deleted phrases except in one case (noted below) where Jarrell found no alternative to the word he struck.

1.   Jarrell writes to Mary, in a letter dated 27 February 1952: "I have a funny beginning—meaning amusing *and* queer—to my first Auden lecture (don't worry, it doesn't go on so) that I can't resist copying out for you. I'll bet the people think—and many unapprovingly, I'm afraid—'I've never heard such a beginning to a lecture.' It begins: Imagine a man on a desert island . . . " There follows the surviving beginning to lecture 1, in slightly more elaborate (hence almost certainly earlier) form. The chief difference subsists in a digression that explains how Auden's collected works got to the desert island, via a shipwrecked American professor headed for the University of Hawai'i, where the professor meant to do research on Auden: "by good fortune it was the research material, and not he, that was washed ashore."

2.   Geoffrey Grigson (1905–1985), English poet and critic, founded and edited *New Verse* (1933–1939), an important venue for Auden, Stephen Spender, and other poets of the British 1930s.

3.   Actually T. H. Huxley, in his essay "Biogenesis and Abiogenesis": "But the great tragedy of Science—the slaying of a beautiful hypothesis by an ugly fact—which is so constantly being enacted under the eyes of philosophers, was played, almost immediately, for the benefit of Buffon and Needham." Huxley, *Discourses Biological*

and Geological (New York: D. Appleton, 1909), 247. Francis Galton related the anecdote Jarrell seems to remember: "Spencer, during a pause in conversation at dinner at the Athenaeum, said, 'You would little think it, but I once wrote a tragedy.' Huxley answered promptly, 'I know the catastrophe.' Spencer declared it was impossible, for he had never spoken about it before then. Huxley insisted. Spencer asked what it was. Huxley replied, 'A beautiful theory, killed by a nasty, ugly little fact.' " Francis Galton, *Memories of My Life* (1908; New York: AMS Press, 1974), 258.

4. Auden, *Letter to Lord Byron*, part 4, includes the lines "You must ask me who / Have written just as I'd have liked to do. / I stop to listen, and the names I hear / Are those of Firbank, Potter, Carroll, Lear" (*EA*, 190).

5. For most of this paragraph about Auden's influences ("Auden has been attacked . . . real or essential Rilke"), two overlapping TS pages exist. The earlier and slightly longer TS page (the one I have not used) contains additional examples of Auden's models ("parodies of 'Locksley Hall' " for example), which Jarrell would use in his third lecture instead. For "An ordinary poet . . . think of Swinburne," I have used MS in preference to TS here, since MS is evidently later; I return to TS at "Our castaway" and follow it to the end of the TS, "rescuers came for," after which the surviving MS is clear and consistent to the end of the lecture.

6. Yeats "offered to spend what remained of life explaining and piecing together those scattered sentences. 'No,' was the answer. 'we have come to give you metaphors for poetry.' " W. B. Yeats, *A Vision* (1938; New York: Macmillan, 1969), 8. Jarrell used the same quotation to conclude his earlier essay on W. B. Yeats; see Jarrell, *Kipling, Auden, and Co.* (New York: Farrar, Straus and Giroux, 1980), 100.

7. John Dryden wrote, of Chaucer's *Canterbury Tales*, " 'Tis sufficient to say according to the Proverb, that here is God's Plenty." *Essays of John Dryden*, ed. W. P. Ker, 2 vols. (New York: Russell and Russell, 1961), 2:262.

8. A reference to Robinson Jeffers; see, for example, Jeffers's poem "Rock and Hawk." Jarrell may also be thinking of Robert Frost's "Into My Own": "They would not find me changed from him they knew— / Only more sure of all I thought was true." *The Poetry of Robert Frost*, ed. Edward Connery Lathem (New York: Henry Holt, 1979), 5.

9. "My writing has all . . . leave-taking from you." Franz Kafka, *Letter to His Father*, trans. E. Kaiser and E. Wilkins (1953; reprint, New York: Schocken, 1973), 87. "All, therefore, that has been confessed by me, consists of fragments of a great confession." J. W. von Goethe, *The Autobiography of Johann Wolfgang von Goethe (Dichtung und Warheit)*, trans. John Oxenford (New York: Horizon, 1969), 305. "Goethe was . . . in spite of the abundance of autobiographical records, a careful concealer." Sigmund Freud, "Address Delivered in the Goethe House" (1930), *The Standard Edition of the Complete Psychological Works of Sigmund Freud*, trans. and ed. James Strachey et al., vol. 21 (London: Hogarth, 1961), 211.

10. Jarrell likely has in mind Freud's well-known paragraphs, in *Civilization and Its Discontents*, comparing the human psyche to Rome: in the psyche, Freud writes, "nothing that has once come into existence will have passed away and all the earlier phases of development continue to exist alongside the latest one." *The Freud Reader*, ed. Peter Gay (New York: Norton, 1989), 726.

11. Jarrell refers here to "Freud to Paul: The Stages of Auden's Ideology," published in *Partisan Review* in fall 1945—the basis for lecture five.

12. Here the MS additions to p. 5 (5a . . . 5d) end, and the lecture continues with MS p. 6; the discussion of "Auden's new book," *Nones*, which this paragraph promises would not take place until Jarrell's fourth lecture.

13. The MS reads "important, he plainly".

14. "Son . . . dream": these lines from "The earth turns over . . . " read, correctly, "I, their author, stand between these dreams, / Son of a nurse and doctor, loaned a room" (*EA*, 145). Jarrell's misquotation reflects a printing error in British editions of *Look, Stranger!* (1935) (called, in America, *On This Island*); thanks to Edward Mendelson for this information. Later versions of the poem delete the second of those two lines (see Auden, *CP*, 123). Wolfgang Köhler (1987–1967): cofounder of the Gestalt school of psychology, author of (among many other books) *Gestalt Psychology* (1947) and *The Place of Value in a World of Fact* (1938); Jarrell had read Köhler as part of his Vanderbilt training in experimental psychology, and he recommended Köhler's work in his 1942 essay "Levels and Opposites." Karl Lashley (1890–1958): experimental psychologist known for his work with rat brains; now considered a founder of neuropsychology.

15. "any Prot . . . kneeling"; misquoted from *Letter to Lord Byron*, part 4: "I know a Prot / Will never really kneel, but only squat" (*EA*, 191). "hymn tunes": see *Letter to Lord Byron*, part 4: "Out of my hours of strumming most of them / Pass playing hymn tunes" (*EA*, 189). "If Wystan . . . angels": Isherwood actually wrote "When we collaborate, I have to keep a sharp eye on him—or down flop the characters on their knees . . . another constant danger is that of interruption by angel-voices. If Auden had his way he would turn every play into a cross between grand opera and high mass." "Some Notes on Auden's Early Poetry," *New Verse* (November 1937): 4–9; repr., Monroe Spears, ed., *Auden: A Collection of Critical Essays* (Englewood Cliffs, N.J.: Prentice-Hall, 1964), 10–14, quotation at 10.

16. Leon Trotsky's laudatory 1933–35 review of Louis-Ferdinand Celine's novel *Journey to the End of the Night* does not contain the phrase, nor does his later discussion of Celine's "hateful attitude towards life": see *Leon Trotsky on Literature and Art*, ed. Paul N. Siegel (New York: Pathfinder, 1970), 191–204, 231–32.

17. *EA*, 39.

18. "The Immanent Will that stirs and urges everything." Thomas Hardy ("The Convergence of the Twain"), *Complete Poems*, ed. James Gibson (New York: Macmillan, 1976), 307.

19. *EA*, 44–45. Jarrell's text reads "Joy is mine not yours to have come so far, / quote a good deal from page 10, *Poems*"; the rest of the quotation (continuing the poem to the end of the stanza, after which Venus stops describing herself and starts to describe "you") represents a best guess.

20. *EA*, 30.

21. A. E. Housman, "Epitaph on an Army of Mercenaries," in *Collected Poems of A. E. Housman* (New York: Holt, Rinehart and Winston, 1965), 144; *EA*, 30.

22. Both quotations from Auden, *Paid on Both Sides*. The first is accurate; the second would read, correctly, "manors mortgaged twice to pay for love" (*EA*, 11, 7).

23. *EA*, 144.

24. Here the MS reads "return to that ~~togetherness~~ synonym," with "synonym" written above the struck-out word (but no synonym offered). Compare Jarrell's later essay on Christina Stead: "go back far enough and which of us knew where he ended and Mother and Father and Brother and Sister began? The singular subject in its

objective universe has evolved from that original composite entity—half subjective, half objective, having its own ways and laws and language, its own life and its own death—the family." Jarrell, *The Third Book of Criticism* (New York: Farrar, Straus and Giroux, 1969), 3.

25. Goethe, *Faust* book 1, part 1, scene 1 ("Night"); for Jarrell's later translation, see his version of *Faust I* (New York: Farrar, Straus and Giroux, 1976), 35.

26. Correctly, "Them cannot mean to now," from *Paid on Both Sides; EA,* 11.

27. *EA,* 85 (from *The Orators*); earlier parts of this sentence represent Jarrell's memorial paraphrase of Auden's longer passage about the Uncle's eyes (84–85).

28. Jarrell wrote in the margin of this paragraph: "Change."

29. *EA,* 39. All quotations from this point to the end of the lecture draw on poem 24 in *Poems* (1930) (later titled "1929"), *EA,* 37–40; "Easter 1929" is Jarrell's mistaken conflation of Auden's title with the first line of the poem.

30. The MS here includes the deleted sentence, "Then Auden take[s] one of Chekhov's statements and makes a rhetorical but still-effective paraphrase of it," and the deleted note "quote Chekhov."

31. Assuming Jarrell gave the lecture as it survives in draft, rather than making later (now lost) revisions, it likely ended with his reading aloud the whole of "Easter 1929," *EA,* 37–40. The lecture proper ends here; the final page concludes with the notations "Read 'Easter 1929' // probably quote / 'Easter 1929' / first then have / paraphrase-summary / and a few more / comments"—an indication (like the incomplete TS) that Jarrell regarded as a draft what turned out to be the final version.

Lecture 2

This lecture consists of eighteen pages of continuous TS and presents no textual problems; it and the following lecture (lecture 3) adapt Jarrell's article "Changes of Attitude and Rhetoric in Auden's Poetry," which appeared in the autumn 1941 Southern Review. Heavily (sometimes illegibly) marked-up copies of the printed article's first eight pages accompany the TS of lecture 2; though lectures 2 and 3 sometimes follow the 1941 article quite closely, a complete account of the

differences between them would take up more space than practicable in a readers'
edition. "Changes" appeared in The Third Book of Criticism *(New York:*
Farrar, Straus and Giroux, 1969) and again in No Other Book *(New York:*
HarperCollins, 1999); interested readers may compare the 1941 article to the
1952 lectures reproduced here.

1. Dissenting from Freud, Georg Groddeck (*The Book of the It*) consid-
    ered all bodily illness psychosomatic, believing that particular
    medical problems, from cancer to eyestrain, arose from neuroses
    or other psychological disorders. Hints of a similar doctrine ap-
    pear in the teachings of the educator (and unlicensed analyst)
    Homer Lane, hence in the ideas of John Layard, the former pa-
    tient of Lane's whom Auden knew in Berlin: see Humphrey Car-
    penter, *W. H. Auden: A Biography* (London: Allen and Unwin, 1981)
    or Edward Mendelson, *Early Auden* (Cambridge, Mass.: Harvard
    University Press, 1981), esp. 55–57, for detailed accounts.
2. The Russian plant biologist T. D. Lysenko (1898–1976) rejected
    standard genetics, maintaining instead that organisms could pass
    on acquired characteristics; under Stalin, Lysenko's theories dom-
    inated Soviet biology.
3. *EA*, 239.
4. "Son . . . dream": see lecture 1, note 14.
5. *EA*, 53–54.
6. Auden, *CP*, 261.
7. Auden, *CP*, 255.
8. "The whole theory of Marx is the application of the theory of de-
    velopment . . . to modern capitalism. . . . Marx treats the question
    of communism in the same way as a naturalist would pose the
    question of the development, say, of a new biological variety, once
    he knew that it had originated in such and such a way and was
    changing in such and such a definite direction." V. I. Lenin, *State
    and Revolution*, chap. 5, section 1, in Lenin, *Marx Engels Marxism*
    (translator uncredited) (Moscow: Progress, 1975), 80–81.
9. *EA*, 44; Auden, *CP*, 43.
10. *EA*, 42.
11. *EA*, 150. The MS places quote marks (wrongly but understandably
    given Auden's difficult grammar) after "lies."
12. *EA*, 149; Auden, *CP*, 124 ("Two Climbs") preserves the later ver-
    sion ("sad and useless").

13. Sir James Jeans (1877–1946), English astronomer and science writer; his popular works include *The Universe Around Us* (1929).

14. The quoted passage reads, correctly, "with all the assurance of the non-airman" (*EA*, 78). As some of his Princeton audience would have known, Jarrell—though he never flew combat missions—served in the Army Air Force during the Second World War; for several months he ran a flight simulator, training the future members of bomber crews in "celestial navigation." His best-known poems about the war almost all involve airplanes or airmen, among them "Losses," "Eighth Air Force," and "The Death of the Ball Turret Gunner."

15. Both the lecture TS and the *Southern Review* article (along with its reprinting in *The Third Book of Criticism*) read "Owens rhymes"; Jarrell must have meant "Owen rhymes" or "Owenseque rhymes," i.e., half-rhymes, matching consonants but not vowels, such as introduced in the poetry of Wilfred Owen, and taken up frequently in early Auden. Jarrell reviewed Owen's *Poems* admiringly in 1950; see *Kipling, Auden, and Co.* (New York: Farrar, Straus and Giroux, 1980), 169.

16. *EA*, 76.

17. G. A. Henty (1932–1902): English author of many adventure stories for and about boys.

18. "It is of great importance to study the various strategies of 'prayer' by which men seek to solve their conflicts, since such material should give us needed insight into the processes of prayer ('symbolic action,' 'linguistic action,' 'implicit commands to audience and self') in its many secular aspects, not generally considered 'prayer' at all." Kenneth Burke, *The Philosophy of Literary Form* (1941; Berkeley: University of California Press, 1973), 313.

19. *Plays*, 279.

20. *Plays*, 97–98.

21. *EA*, 455, 247 (correctly, "Show an affirming flame").

22. "It is the same machinery, in the fearful case of Swift, that betrays not consciousness of the audience but a doubt of which he may himself have been unconscious. 'Everything spiritual and valuable has a gross and revolting parody, very similar to it, with the same name. Only unremitting judgment can distinguish between them'; he set out to simplify the work of judgment by giving a complete set of obscene puns for it." William Empson, *Some Versions of Pastoral* (1935; New York: New Directions, 1974).

23. Gresham's Law: "bad money drives out good." (Originally in eco-
nomics, the principle that where two forms of coin circulate with
the same declared legal value, but different values as metal [e.g.,
silver and gold], people will conduct transactions with the lesser-
valued coin [the silver], and hoard the greater [the gold].)

24. Sir Joshua Reynolds, "Johnson Against Garrick," in *Portraits*, ed.
F. W. Hilles (London: Methuen, 1952), 92–94, quotation at 94.

25. *EA*, 34.

26. The American literary and political journal *New Masses*
(1926–1942) published Marxist criticism and "proletarian writ-
ing," as defined by its editor-in-chief Mike Gold.

27. Jarrell's TS places a question mark here; "Changes" has a full stop.

28. "The large extent to which psycho-analysis coincides with the phi-
losophy of Schopenhauer . . . is not to be traced to my acquaintance
with his teaching. I read Schopenhauer very late in my life." Sig-
mund Freud, "An Autobiographical Study," in *The Standard Edition of
the Complete Psychological Works of Sigmund Freud*, trans. and ed. James
Strachey et al., vol. 20 (London: Hogarth, 1959), 59–60.

29. *EA*, 212.

30. The TS has "I do not want to write more" deleted in blue ink, but
nothing to replace it; "a fifth lecture will explain," however, is a
handwritten addition, completing the TS's fragmentary "mere re-
minders that tried to explain it in detail."

31. *EA*, 246.

32. Shakespeare, *2 Henry IV*, 4.5.182–85: "God knows, my son, / By
what bypaths and indirect crook'd ways / I met this crown, and I
myself know well / How troublesome it sat upon my head."

33. Elstir, the painter, befriends the young Marcel in Proust's *Remem-
brance of Things Past*, and delivers this speech near the end of *A l'om-
bre des jeunes filles et fleurs* ("Within a Budding Grove"). Jarrell cites
C. K. Scott Moncrieff's translation. Proust, *Remembrance of Things
Past*, trans. C. K. Scott Moncrieff (New York: Random House,
1934), 1:649. Jarrell cited Proust to similarly authoritative effect at
the end of "The Obscurity of the Poet": "But this has been said,
better than it is ever again likely to be said, by the greatest of the
writers of this century, Marcel Proust; and I should like to finish
this lecture by quoting his sentences . . . " There follows a long
paragraph inspired, in *A la recherche*, by Elstir's death. *Poetry and the
Age* (London: Faber and Faber, 1953), 35.

34. "Greek homosexuality in Naomi Mitchison": for example, the male lovers in Mitchison's *The Corn King and the Spring Queen* (1930).
35. *Plays*, 224.
36. *EA*, 88.
37. *EA*, 105.
38. Friedrich Engels, *Anti-Dühring*, trans. Emile Burns, ed. C. P. Dutt (1939; New York: International Publishers, 1966), 221. Engels's attacks on Dühring's insistence on "unity" perhaps have faint echoes in Jarrell's descriptions (in lecture 5 here) of Auden's insistent monism, composed (like this passage) in the early 1940s, when Jarrell was still reading Marxist theory; see Engels, *Anti-Dühring*, 48–49.
39. *EA*, 71.
40. See, for example, Stephen Spender, *Poems* (New York: Random House, 1934), 10, 12, 35.
41. *EA*, 40.

Lecture 3

This lecture consists of twenty-two pages of TS with MS inserts and without page numbers, most of it clearly continuous but with a few gaps and illogical transitions that suggest that the existing order (the order of pages at the Berg Collection) cannot be right. Notes to the body of this lecture explain my editorial decisions as to the most likely order. Much of the lecture adapts the second half of "Changes of Attitude and Rhetoric" (see lecture 2, note 1); other parts adapt Jarrell's review of Auden's The Age of Anxiety, *first printed in* The Nation, *18 October 1947, and reprinted in* Kipling, Auden, and Co. *(New York: Farrar, Straus and Giroux, 1980), 145–46.*

1. *EA*, 204; *Plays*, 206; *EA*, 111, 217; *Plays*, 280; *CP*, 249; *EA*, 203; perhaps *EA*, 206 ("a sterile dragon"; poem excluded from *CP*); *CP*, 251; *EA*, 143; *EA*, 229; *EA*, 136; *Plays*, 279; *EA*, 155, 217 (correctly "incurious").
2. *EA*, 155 (correctly "of the pier").
3. This paragraph break coincides with the end of the TS page; the order of TS pages at the Berg Collection continues with "Page after page the poem keeps saying . . ." That page and the next TS

page (with its MS additions) belong to Jarrell's discussion of *The Age of Anxiety* and are clearly out of place; I have replaced them where they seem to belong (as indicated both by the logic of the lecture and by the order of Jarrell's 1947 review), picking up here two TS pages later, with "This sort of thing," which follows the order of paragraphs in "Changes of Attitude and Rhetoric."

4. We have not located "dumb and violent"; for the other quotations, *EA*, 152, 158, 160; *CP*, 257; *EA*, 115, 157.
5. *EA*, 164, 203, 217, 159, 243, 222 (correctly "Money"), 148.
6. *EA*, 165.
7. *EA*, 157, 108.
8. *EA*, 456.
9. A passage from *The Orators* (*EA*, 71); later editions restored Auden's noun "bugger," which asterisks obscure in Jarrell's edition (whichever one he is using).
10. *EA*, 165; *Plays*, 212; *CP*, 203, 215 (both from "New Year Letter").
11. "Pascal," *EA*, 451–53. Jarrell had admired the poem on its first appearance in a 1939 *Southern Review*, writing to Peter Taylor "Isn't Auden's poem on Pascal—all but the end? Just wonderful? I hope you and Cal [Robert Lowell] have read it with love and care." "Letters to Peter and Eleanor Ross Taylor," *Yale Review* 91, no. 1 (2003): 69–77, quotation at 71.
12. *EA*, 238, 237.
13. *EA*, 229 (correctly "rooks in the college garden / Like agile babies"; *Collected Poetry* 1945 has the same reading, though Auden later altered the line to "rooks . . . Still talk like agile babies," *CP*, 147); *EA*, 243.
14. *EA*, 115, 236.
15. *EA*, 238.
16. Rainer Maria Rilke, *Poems*, trans. J. B. Leishman (London: Hogarth, 1934), 43.
17. *EA*, 239, 154, 151, 136, 152 (correctly "lucky to Love").
18. *EA*, 456.
19. *EA*, 241–43.
20. *EA*, 241.
21. Jarrell's handwritten note here says: "read plain, then read italicized."
22. *EA*, 239.

23. And on *CP*, 227–28; in this extended passage from "New Year Letter" "Those limestone moors that stretch from BROUGH / To HEXHAM and the ROMAN WALL" give Auden "my symbol for us all" (*CP*, 227).

24. *Plays*, 402.

25. Most of the items in this list—"Locksley Hall," "Bryan, Bryan, Bryan" (properly "Bryan, Bryan, Bryan, Bryan," a poem by Vachel Lindsay)—occur in the earlier TS drafts of lecture 1, in Jarrell's list of Auden's poetic models: Jarrell seems to have deleted them from that list in order to use them in this one.

26. *EA*, 143, 237; *CP*, 274.

27. *EA*, 245, 460 (correctly "some Hitlerian monster," also the reading in *Collected Poetry* 1945).

28. Poems "published for the first time in book form" in *Collected Poetry* 1945 were marked by asterisks besides their titles (3).

29. *CP*, 318–19.

30. Friedrich Nietzsche, *The Birth of Tragedy*, trans. Walter Kauffman (New York: Random House, 1967), 85 (section 12).

31. "As soon as we take the notion of craft seriously, it is perfectly obvious that art cannot be any kind of craft." R. G. Collingwood, *The Principles of Art* (Oxford: Clarendon, 1938), 26.

32. TS page ends in the middle of this sentence, at "Auden's" (thus confirming that the *Age of Anxiety* material begins here).

33. *CP*, 457; properly, "snap / Verdicts" (also "Verdicts" in *The Age of Anxiety* [New York: Random House, 1946]).

34. The Berg Collection page order ends the lecture here; the pages I place later do not only follow logically here, but also follow the paragraph order of Jarrell's 1947 review, which continues from the block quote (ending "slight / Unfriendly fry . . . ") into a paragraph beginning "Page after page the poem keeps saying . . . "

35. Gerard Manley Hopkins, "Spelt from Sibyl's Leaves," in *The Poems of Gerard Manley Hopkins*, ed. W. H. Gardner and N. H. Mackenzie (London: Oxford University Press, 1967), 97–98. Jarrell may also be suggesting that Auden derives the accentual metre in *Age* partly from Hopkins's example.

36. Text from the start of this sentence ("Later I met") to "beneath him, really?" represent Jarrell's handwritten additions to the TS.

37. Stanley Edgar Hyman, *The Armed Vision* (1948; New York: Vintage,

1955) set out "to study the nature of modern critical method as ex-
emplified by selected contemporary critics," among them Yvor
Winters, T. S. Eliot, Caroline Spurgeon, William Empson, and
Kenneth Burke (viii).

38. *CP*, 464.
39. TS here ends a few lines before the end of the page, supporting
my decision to take this sentence as the final one in the third lec-
ture. The page order at the Berg Collection continues with the
page beginning "This sort of thing is not Auden's discovery."

Lecture 4

*This lecture presents remarkable textual problems. The present text combines the
seventh and the fourth of the nine folders corresponding to the Auden lectures in
the Berg collection. The first part of the lecture as printed here, the material on
"Spain 1937"—from "When one thinks about . . . " to "things that are left"—
survives in the Berg Collection as the seventh folder; it comprises MS pages num-
bered consecutively from 1 to 12. Internal evidence both at the end of this MS
and in the MS preserved in the fourth Berg folder (and described below) strong-
ly suggests that Jarrell spoke on "Spain" (hence on the faults of Auden's "mid-
dle" period), then segued into a discussion of Auden's virtues. Lecture 3 had apol-
ogized for discussing* The Age of Anxiety *out of chronological order; if
Jarrell resumed a chronological discussion at the start of lecture 4, he would have
begun with the Auden of the late 1930s, with "Spain 1937" as a famously rep-
resentative text. The "Spain" material concludes with alternative transition sen-
tences; either of the alternatives in the MS could introduce what has survived as
lecture 4. Moreover, the emendations in pen to this MS correspond (both in sub-
stance and in ink color and nib size) to the emendations Jarrell made to the MS
in folder four (they are blue and concern Nones).*

*The rest of the lecture as printed here corresponds to the MS preserved in the
fourth of the nine folders in Berg, and labeled there as lecture 4. This material,
covering Auden's poetry generally, consists of four TS pages and eight MS
pages numbered consecutively (1 through 8). The first three TS pages follow
part of the MS, from "Auden is not only extremely intelligent" to "Sydney
Smith," with many small changes suggesting later revision for print (for exam-
ple, removing the reference to "my hearers"). Another TS page placed, in the Berg
Collection order, after MS p. 8 duplicates the MS paragraph which follows TS*

p. 3, adding the parenthetical sentence about The Shield of Achilles *in note 10 below. These differences prove the TS not only later than the MS but probably later than the lectures' delivery, and I follow MS throughout.*

*A second set of MS pages follow, numbered consecutively 1–15; these pages describe Auden's most recent work—as of the spring of 1952—*Nones *(1951). As with lecture 3 and lecture 6, Jarrell appears to have written this lecture in separate units, combining them on delivery. Jarrell made handwritten revisions on both the first and the second sets of MS pages in several inks, both blue and black; while some of the revisions pertain to* Nones, *and hence to the lecture as likely delivered, others revise the lecture so that it describes* The Shield of Achilles *(1955). Jarrell would use some of these amended passages in his published review of* The Shield of Achilles *(*Yale Review, *summer 1955;* Kipling, Auden, and Co. *[New York: Farrar, Straus and Giroux, 1980], 226–30)—other revisions and marginal notes suggest that Jarrell was preparing, either in 1955 or later, an integrated essay on Auden's recent work, or on his best work, using both parts of this 1952 lecture. The task of editing this part of the lecture thus involves distinguishing between Jarrell's revisions of 1951 and 1952 and his revisions of 1955 (or later); where neither the color and kind of ink nor the content of a handwritten revision makes such a distinction possible, I have accepted the revision unless otherwise noted.*

The title on TS p. 1 reads both "lecture four" (crossed out, probably by Jarrell) and, in Jarrell's hand, "Auden's best poems": I reject "Auden's best poems" as a title for the lecture, both because other lectures lack titles, and because "Auden's best poems" does not describe the lecture as it stands; most likely Jarrell crossed out "lecture four" and attached the title "Auden's best poems" during later revision.

If Jarrell indeed revised lecture 4 for a later essay, abandoned the revisions before completing the essay, and then cannibalized that MS for his review of The Shield of Achilles, *that series of revisions would explain not only the series of emendations to the MS and TS in folder four, but also the manner in which the material in folder seven (on "Spain") became separated from the material in folder four (assuming they were originally one lecture). Neither an essay on "The Best of Auden," nor an essay on Auden's post-1940 work, nor a review of* The Shield of Achilles *would have any use for Jarrell's critique of "Spain"; Jarrell would have put the "Spain" material aside, in a separate folder—where it remained.*

1. "If the executant artists . . . including the chorus, treated the work with no consideration for its special or poetic subject matter, but rather as disembodied, or 'pure,' theater, just 'wow' material, that is exactly what the composer himself has done, what his score invites

and asks for." Virgil Thomson, *Music Right and Left* (1951; New York: Greenwood, 1969), 72–73. The final movement of Beethoven's Fifth Symphony, Thomson wrote earlier, "is a skillful piece of pure theater, a playing upon audience psychology that has for its final effect, along with the expression of some perfectly real content, the provoking of applause for its own sake." Thomson, *The Art of Judging Music* (1947; New York: Greenwood, 1969), 303.

2. *EA*, 210–12. MS has here "Read pg 81, *Collected Poems*." "Spain 1937" occurs on p. 181 of *Collected Poetry* 1945; evidently a pen-stroke is missing. (Page 81 has the second half of "Oxford.") Note that Jarrell reads "Spain 1937," the version which appears in *Collected Poetry* 1945 and in *Another Time*, not "Spain," the earlier and slightly longer pamphlet version which contained an infamous line about "necessary murder," and which occasioned George Orwell's attack.

3. Jarrell has crossed out "in Auden's new book" and added "in *Nones*"—apparently a post-1952 change.

4. The MS includes, here, Jarrell's sketch of an hourglass.

5. MS reads, here, "(Read both)."

6. *Journey's End*: the 1929 play by R. C. Sherriff, set during the First World War.

7. Compare the opening of Rilke's Eighth Duino Elegy: "Mit allen Augen sieht die Kreatur / das Offene [All other creatures look into the Open / with their whole eyes]." Rainer Maria Rilke, *Duino Elegies and the Sonnets to Orpheus*, trans. A. Poulin Jr., (Boston: Houghton Mifflin, 1977), 54–55.

8. A later addition in black ink (like the ink used in the 1955 additions to lecture 4) reads here "or Auden's later 'We are left alone with our past' in *Nones*." Jarrell misquotes the last sentence in Henry James's *Turn of the Screw*: "We were alone with the quiet day, and his little heart, dispossessed, had stopped." Henry James, *Complete Stories, 1892–1898* (New York: Library of America, 1996), 740.

9. "Whom . . . misled": Goethe, "Proverbs in Rhyme," trans.Isider Schneider, in *The Permanent Goethe*, ed. Thomas Mann (New York: Dial, 1948), 614. Jarrell could have found "The Carousel" (1907) and letters concerning the poem in *Translations from the Poetry of Rainer Maria Rilke*, trans. M. D. Herder Norton (New York: Norton, 1938), 172, 243–44. Rilke wrote that when he read to an audience, "except for the Carousel nothing was even picked up" (244).

10. This sentence appears in the "Spain" MS as one of two cancelled alternatives immediately after "are left." The last MS page continues with cancelled sentences in two parallel columns: on the left, "But these faults are the faults of one of the best of living poets; after having talked so much about, I should like to talk for a while, quite generally, about Auden's virtues"; on the right, "Now write about faults of middle period, read *Dover 1937* and one or two more; say you'll read some good ones from this period in last lecture," with the addition (marked by an arrow), "Of course faults one of best of living poets—virtues *force* themselves on us; remarkably *effective* poems, God knows." I take the sentence on the left as later than the sentence on the right; it suggests that this material on "Spain 1937" leads into what the Berg Collection preserves as lecture 4.

11. "Gleam, light up, sparkle" appear in TS as alternatives, with none crossed out.

12. "Every author, as far as he is great and at the same time *original*, has had the task of *creating* the taste by which he is to be enjoyed." William Wordsworth, "Essay, Supplementary to the Preface" [to *Poems*, 1815]; *The Prose Works of William Wordsworth*, vol. 3, ed. W. J. B. Owen and Jane Worthington Smyser (Oxford: Clarendon, 1974), 80. "It was Beethoven's Quartets themselves (the Twelfth, Thirteenth, Fourteenth and Fifteenth) that devoted half a century to forming, fashioning and enlarging a public for Beethoven's Quartets." Marcel Proust, *Remembrance of Things Past*, vol. 1, trans. C. K. Scott Moncrieff (New York: Random House, 1943), 405.

13. MS has the ungrammatical "roaming through it seeking."

14. Stendhal, *The Charterhouse of Parma* (1839), chapter 26.

15. Here the three consecutive TS pages end.

16. TS adds here the parenthetical sentence: "(But this has changed until [in] his last book, *The Shield of Achilles*, he enjoys his favorite landscapes a good deal more than he enjoys the people who inhabit them: people dry out faster than landscapes, in a pigeon-hole.)"

17. Compare, to this apparently unsympathetic comment, the biographer Richard Davenport-Hines's decision that Auden had "difficulty in appreciating the individuality of other people. . . . Until about 1946 he tended to treat other people like types." *Auden* (New York: Pantheon, 1995), 46.

18. *CP*, 381. TS here adds a brief comment on Western difficulty in distinguishing Chinese faces (and vice versa), and then ends.
19. G. S. Fraser attacked the same passage, for the same reasons: see Fraser, "The Career of W. H. Auden", in Monroe Spears, ed., *Auden: A Collection of Critical Essays* (Englewood Cliffs, N.J.: Prentice-Hall, 1964), 81–104, quotation at 90.
20. Here a deleted passage reads: "When you compare Auden's poems with that of a wonderful specialized poet like Dylan Thomas, who by now writes only a kind of sexual pastoral about imaginary unmoral human animals, you realize the difference between a very complete half-poet and an incomplete whole one." Several lines of notes follow. Jarrell used this distinction between a "partial" or "specialized" poet, like Thomas, and a "complete" one in his writings on Frost: "Frost is that rare thing, a complete or representative poet, and not one of the brilliant partial poets who do justice, far more than justice, to a portion of reality, and leave the rest of things forlorn": "there is more sexuality [in 'The Pauper Witch of Grafton'] than in several hothouses full of Dylan Thomas" (*Poetry and the Age* [1953; reprint, Gainesville: University Press of Florida, 2001], 68, 62).
21. Here the first eight MS pages end; Jarrell's note here—evidently made in 1955 or in a later revision—reads "? Then use part about *Shield of Achilles* and *Nones*." The remainder of the lecture follows the fifteen consecutive MS pages numbered 1–15.
22. *CP*, 634.
23. *SP*, 224.
24. *EA*, 212.
25. MS reads "Read *Nones*, page 55"; page 55 of *Nones* (New York: Random House, 1950) consists of the first and almost all of the second stanza of the poem "Nones" (up to "It was a monster with one red eye"), later incorporated into the sequence *Horae Canonicae* (*CP*, 634). More likely Jarrell read the whole poem, which differs in some punctuation from the *CP* version; I give the *Nones* punctuation here.
26. Jarrell misquotes, slightly, "Letter to Lord Byron": Auden actually wrote that he "Must hear in silence till I turn my toes up, / 'It's such a pity Wystan never grows up.' " *EA*, 190.
27. These added sentences (in black ink) replace these deleted sentences: "People used to complain heartily about Eliot's 'Why

should the agéd eagle stretch his wings'; they would subtract 1888
from 1927 and say, 'Now is that old?' There seemed to them some-
thing of a pose in Eliot's line. Nobody has said anything of the sort
about Auden's." Compare, in Jarrell's review of *The Shield of Achilles*:
"Wystan has grown up; has grown old—as old as Talleyrand, as
Disraeli, as that 'tired old diplomat' who's become a stock figure in
the poems. People used to resent Eliot's 'Why should the aged ea-
gle stretch his wings?' but Auden has got over on the shady side
of so much, has become so convincingly old, so irrevocably, inex-
orably middle-aged, that we wouldn't resent his telling us that he
is the Wandering Jew" (*Kipling, Auden, and Co.*, 228).

28. *CP*, 583.
29. *CP*, 204.
30. *CP*, 336.
31. The poem is Housman, "The Welsh Marches, " in *Collected Poems of
A. E. Housman* (New York: Holt, Rinehart and Winston, 1965),
44–45.
32. Lloyd Frankenberg, compiler, *Pleasure Dome: An Audible Anthology of
Modern Poetry Read by the Creators*, Columbia Records, 1949.
33. Handwritten additions alter and add to the previous sentence so
that it reads "about most of *Nones*, a complacent frivolity about
most of *The Shield of Achilles*, and this . . . ". Another added and then
cancelled passage here reads, "If a stranger to their work were to
read Auden's *Nones* and then to read Lowell's new book, *The Mills
of the Kavanaghs*, and then to read what was published about them,
and were then told that Auden is a major poet, one of the great-
est of living poets, and that Lowell is a fine young American poet
of great promise—if our imaginary reader were told this, he would
have to shake himself in bewilderment, and think, 'No, some-
body's got mixed up, they've got it backwards, *something's* wrong.' "
Jarrell appears to have cancelled this sentence about Lowell in
1951 or 1952; in 1955 (or later) Jarrell altered the previous sen-
tence, "There is a real . . . of 44" to read "*Paid on Both Sides* at 23, at
48 is publishing *The Shield of Achilles*," and then cancelled the entire
sentence. Another note after "disquieting ring" reads "Stop about
here, then on to later page"; I take these directions as probably
dating from 1955.
34. *CP*, 332, *Nones*, 32–33 (unchanged). MS reads "Read."
35. MS reads "(read p. 52, *Nones*—first 3 stanzas)" (rather than copy-

ing out the three stanzas here). The poem reappeared with differ-
ent punctuation in *CP*, 614.

36. MS reads "(read all of page 59)" rather than copying out the poem;
this text presents the first eight stanzas of "A Household," i.e., all
of page 59 in *Nones*. "A Household" also appears in *CP*, 618.

37. Jarrell's handwritten note here note reads: "Start about here,
from early page 12"; the first few lines of the following MS page
are crossed. I take these directions, too, as probably dating from
1955.

38. Frost's poem "The Oven Bird" ends: "The question that he frames
in all but words / Is what to make of a diminished thing." *The Poet-
ry of Robert Frost*, ed. Edward Connery Lathem (New York: Henry
Holt, 1979), 119.

39. *Nones*, 45–46, *CP*, 545–46 with minor changes. The lecture ends
here with the handwritten addition "[several sentences about]";
presumably Jarrell ad-libbed some commentary on "Under Sirius"
before reading the poem aloud.

Lecture 5

*Lecture 5 consists of thirty-five continuous TS pages, unnumbered; it adapts
Jarrell's earlier article "Freud to Paul: the Stages of Auden's Ideology," original-
ly printed in* Partisan Review, *fall 1945, and reprinted in* The Third Book
of Criticism *(New York: Farrar, Straus and Giroux, 1969), 153–90. The
second lecture had promised that the fifth lecture would take up these concerns.
The lecture bears the additional title, or titles, in Jarrell's handwriting, "Freud to
Paul from '28 to '45." Accompanying the TS in Berg folder five are the first two
pages of the* Partisan *"Freud to Paul," very heavily marked up with changes.
A letter to Mary (the associated envelope dated 9 October 1951) confirms that
Jarrell planned this lecture as his fifth: "I've the third lecture virtually done, the
fourth 3/5 done, and the 5th is already done, of course. And I'll have the two
weeks between the 4th and the 6th to write the 6th in" (Berg). The fifth lecture
was "already done, of course" because it adapted a previously published article,
rather than (like the fourth and sixth) being composed largely from scratch.*

1. Goethe, *Faust*, 1:682–83; *CP*, 250 (and see also *Prose2*, 39); quoted
in Freud, "The Ego and the Id," in *The Freud Reader*, ed. Peter Gay
(New York: Norton, 1989), 635.

2. TS: "Here every——- of importance"; "Freud to Paul" (article): "Here everything important".

3. "presents . . . terms": Jarrell quotes Thomas Mann's remark "In our time the destiny of man presents its meanings in political terms," made famous as the epigraph to Yeats's poem "Politics"; *The Collected Works of W. B. Yeats, Vol. I: Poems*, ed. Richard J. Finneran (New York: Macmillan, 1989), 348. Jarrell reacted with hostility to the same remark in "The Pound Affair," written probably in 1949 and 1950: see "The Pound Affair," *Thumbscrew* 14 (1999): 10–15.

4. Jarrell paraphrases the notes to *New Year Letter*: "freedom is a concept of conscious human beings, and is, as Engels defines it, a consciousness of necessity." Auden, *The Double Man* (New York: Random House, 1941), 77. "Hegel was the first to state correctly the relation between freedom and necessity. To him, freedom is the appreciation of necessity. . . . Freedom does not consist in the dream of independence of natural laws, but in the knowledge of those laws, and in the possibility this gives of systematically making them work towards definite ends." Friedrich Engels, *Anti-Duhring*, trans. Emil Burns (1939; New York: International Publishers, 1966), 125.

5. "The relation of man's essential nature to his sinful state cannot be solved within terms of the chronological version of the perfection before the Fall. It is, as it were, a vertical rather than horizontal relation. When the Fall is made an event in history rather than a symbol of an aspect of every historical moment in the life of man, the relation of evil to goodness in that moment is obscured"; "Perfection before the Fall is, in other words, perfection before the act." Reinhold Niebuhr, *The Nature and Destiny of Man*, vol. 1 (1941; New York: Scribner, 1949), 269, 278.

6. *Prose2*, 139.

7. Karl Barth (1886–1968), the Swiss Protestant antiliberal theologian.

8. For example, in Louis Untermeyer, ed., *Modern British Poetry*, fifth ed. (New York: Harcourt, Brace, 1942).

9. TS (following the article "Freud to Paul") reads "presented as Sir Stafford Cripps"; Jarrell has circled both "Churchill" and "Sir Stafford Cripps" in pencil, cancelled "Sir Stafford Cripps" and written over it "Attlee." Following this paragraph, TS preserves the Roman numeral "II." before the next paragraph; this numeral (like the later "III.") represents a carry-over from "Freud to Paul" (see *Third*, 161) and suggests that Jarrell had someone at Princeton type up additions and changes to a marked-up copy of the *Parti-*

san article. Attlee was the Labour prime minister of Great Britain, elected in 1945; Cripps—a name more familiar to Americans in 1945 than in 1952—was a long-serving Labour politician, ambassador to the Soviet Union during the Second World War, and later an architect of Attlee's economic policies.

10. Jarrell writes in the margin beside this sentence: "a little awkward."

11. This definition of "ideology" does not, in fact, appear in Engels's *Anti-Dühring*, but in his correspondence, being taken from Engels's letter to Franz Mehring, 14 July 1893: see Karl Marx and Friedrich Engels, *Selected Correspondence, 1846–1895* (1942; New York: Greenwood/Marxist Library, 1975), 511. (Jarrell would have known—and quoted, probably from memory—an earlier translation, perhaps the Marx-Engels-Lenin Institute edition of Engels's letters, published in English in 1933.)

12. *EA*, 62.

13. Abram Kardiner et al., *The Psychological Frontiers of Society* (New York: Columbia University Press, 1945), 426.

14. Kardiner et al., 425.

15. *EA*, 94.

16. "Intellectual existence, especially for the religious man, is not easy, the believer lies constantly out upon the deep and with seventy thousand fathoms of water under him"; "the religious contradiction: at the same time to lie upon seventy thousand fathoms of water and yet be joyful." Søren Kierkegaard, *Stages on Life's Way*, trans. Walter Lowrie (Princeton, N.J.: Princeton University Press, 1940), 402, 430. See *CP*, 409.

17. The French mathematician Pierre-Simon Laplace (1747–1827) believed that, in principle, a calculator with enough data and the right equations could predict the future behavior of every entity in the universe—a particularly memorable form of philosophical determinism.

18. *Prose2*, 214.

19. The TS continues (following the article "Freud to Paul"): "When, in early 1941, liberal magazines were racking their brains over what to do, to think, or even to write about the war that was perhaps a crusade, and perhaps a struggle of rival imperialisms; the Russia that was perhaps Utopia, a trifle regimented, and perhaps the Companion of Hitler; the world that was, and no perhaps about it, a hopeless mess—suddenly there was a great increase of articles about the situation of the Negro in America. It would take a hard man to look

unsympathetically at so revealing a manifestation of our being." Jarrell has written in the margin, beside this digression: "cut?".

20. "For Europe is absent. This is an island and therefore / Unreal" (*EA*, 203); "Europe is absent: this is an island and should be / a refuge" (*CP*, 150).

21. *EA*, 212. Again, Jarrell quotes "Spain 1937."

22. *CP*, 238 ("New Year Letter").

23. *Prose2*, 113.

24. Beside "anthropological fantasy" Jarrell pencils in "myth."

25. *EA*, 190 (and see lecture 4, note 26).

26. Alfred Tarski (1901–1983) and Gottlob Frege (1848–1925), logicians and founders of twentieth-century analytic philosophy.

27. *EA*, 193, 176 ("Letter to Lord Byron").

28. Jarrell would reuse this joke in his novel, placing Auden's remark about education in the mouth of a self-important anthologist, novelist, and educator, Charles Daudier, modeled in part on Louis Untermeyer, and his own reply in the mouth of another novelist, Gertrude Johnson, modeled in part on Mary McCarthy: Johnson says to Daudier,

> "What you said about the ideal education being manual labor and Greek. Now, I was interested in that. . . . Who said that first?"
>
> Mr. Daudier said that he thought he'd said it first, though he might have read it somewhere else and forgotten; my heart was hardened, and I said: "I think it's Auden." Mr. Daudier looked at me like Pyrrho the Skeptic. Gertrude said, "Yes, that must be right," and gestured towards me, saying, "*He* knows Auden by heart, practically." Then she got back to business: "What you said about manual labor and Greek, that they're the ideal education, that made me think of Cassandra. I mean, when the Greeks captured her and made a slave out of her, she could have cheered herself up by thinking that at least she was going to get an ideal education. And that was so about *any* Greek slave—any slave that was a foreigner to begin with, and didn't know Greek. But there's one thing that bothered me: how could any *Greek* get an ideal education? *They* already knew Greek."

Jarrell, *Pictures from an Institution* (1954; reprint, Chicago: University of Chicago Press, 1986), 243.

Ian Sansom, " 'Flouting Papa': Randall Jarrell and W. H. Auden," in *In Solitude, for Company: W. H. Auden After 1940*, ed. Katherine Bucknell and

Nicholas Jenkins, Auden Studies 3 (Oxford: Clarendon, 1995), 274, also discusses the passage.

29. Perhaps: "I always believe that obedience is dearer to God than . . . sacrifices upon the altar of humanity." Søren Kierkegaard, *Stages on Life's Way*, trans. Walter Lowrie (Princeton, N.J.: Princeton University Press, 1940), 244.

30. "The works of men may always be attractive and seemingly good. It appears nevertheless that they are mortal sins." Martin Luther, "Theses for the Heidelberg Disputation" (1518), in *Martin Luther: Selections from His Writings*, trans. John Dillenberger (New York: Doubleday, 1961), 500–503, quotation at 501.

31. *CP*, 366 ("For the Time Being").

32. Jarrell writes in the margin beside this paragraph: "change a little."

33. *CP*, 354 ("For the Time Being").

34. *CP*, 242 ("New Year Letter").

35. Perhaps Jarrell is remembering, and rephrasing: "The religious dimension of sin is man's rebellion against God, his efforts to usurp the place of God." Reinhold Niebuhr, *The Nature and Destiny of Man*, vol. 1 (1941; New York: Scribner, 1949), 179.

36. *Prose2*, 241.

37. Sigmund Freud, *New Introductory Lectures on Psychoanalysis*, trans. W. J. H. Sprott (New York: Norton, 1933), 150–51, quotation at 149. (Note that this translation—taken from chapter 32—differs from that in the later Standard Edition.)

38. *Prose2*, 242.

39. *CP*, 387 ("For the Time Being").

40. Emphases, and square brackets, here are Jarrell's. "Passive . . . powers": nothing in *EA*, *CP*, or *Prose2* corresponds closely to this quotation, apparently a condensation and misquotation from memory of *Prose2*, 39; for the second set of quotations (about Reinhold Niebuhr), see *Prose2*, 108–9.

41. *Prose2*, 13–15.

42. TS preserves "III." at this paragraph, another carryover from the *Partisan Review* text; see note 9 to this lecture (and *Third*, 185, where Jarrell also promised a future "discussion of the effect on Auden's ideology of Freud, Marx, Paul, Luther, Calvin, Kierkegaard, Kafka, Barth, and Niebuhr"; unsurprisingly, no such article appeared).

43. *Prose2*, 242.

Lecture 6

As with lecture 4, the version presented here represents a conjectural reconstruc-
tion, created by adding other surviving fragments to the obviously incomplete
MS the Berg Collection preserves as lecture 6. The first section of this lecture, a
reading of Paid on Both Sides, *survives in the Berg Collection as folder 8 of*
the nine devoted to the lectures: this MS consists of eleven consecutively numbered
MS pages, followed by five pages of MS notes, numbered 1–4 and 4a. This MS
corresponds to the text here from the start of the lecture to "Yeah, the usual sort
of readers . . . next!" The separate MS that survives as lecture 6 (i.e., folder 6)
makes clear that the material on Paid *was delivered as a part of a lecture (or*
possibly a whole lecture) at some point during the seminars preceding (the rest
of) lecture 6. My decision to place this material here, rather than in any earlier
lecture or as an appendix, has the least textual support of any decision made in
creating this book: I place it here because it was clearly written for oral delivery,
because it seems to belong with Jarrell's discussion of Auden's later long poems,
and because it has no clear place at the start or end of earlier lectures. (Another
possible location for it might be at the start of lecture 2.) As with lecture 4, Jar-
rell may have separated these MSS out from an original unified lecture in order
to use parts of the lecture for his later essay on Auden; he could also have used
the Paid *material for a talk on an unrelated occasion.*

The rest of the lecture corresponds (with additions noted below) to the sixth
of the nine Berg folders. This lecture as the Berg Collection preserves it consists
of 31 consecutive MS pages numbered from 1 to 16, with page 7 followed by
7a . . . 7d, and then 8. MS pages 1–7c use both sides of each page; pages 9–16
are written on verso of a typed compilation of Jarrell's late 1940s and early
1950s poems, perhaps distributed at his 1952 readings. Jarrell (or someone else)
has added to page 1 the title "Auden's Long Poems." These pages cover all of
Auden's long poems (excluding the dramatic collaborations) up to 1952 with
three exceptions: Paid on Both Sides; "For the Time Being"; *and* The Age
of Anxiety, *which Jarrell has already discussed in lecture three. The sixteen*
MS pages also appear unfinished, breaking off in the middle of a discussion of
"The Sea and the Mirror." Sections of lectures on "For the Time Being" and
"The Sea and the Mirror" survive in the Berg Collection in a way which al-
lows for plausible if not definitive reconstruction of the whole lecture; the miss-
ing pieces and their provenance are discussed in notes below. Handwritten revi-
sions suggest that (as with lecture 4) Jarrell began to revise this lecture for
possible book or article publication (which process may also have led to the
scattering of its pieces). As with lecture 4, I have tried to come as close as pos-

sible to the lecture Jarrell actually gave, and so have rejected any revision which obviously dates from after 1952.

1. *EA*, 2. MS has simply an asterisk after "speech of the chorus" and continues to "Immediately afterwards"; he may well have read the rest of the choral speech (extending to "The last transgression of the sea") as well.
2. *EA*, 5. MS does not copy the extended quotation, but instead reads "(* Read page 65, *Sometimes we read a sign* through page 66 *and some were willing* *)." Here and throughout the lecture Jarrell's page numbers for *Paid* correspond to pages in Auden's *Poems* (1934).
3. *EA*, 7. MS does not copy the extended quotation, but instead reads "* Read p 68, *Always the following wind of history*."
4. *EA*, 7. MS does not copy extended quotation, but reads "*Read *the Spring unsettles*, p. 69.*"
5. *EA*, 8. MS does not copy extended quotation, but reads "** Read *Bo* and *Po* on pages 70 and 71 **."
6. *EA*, 11 (omitting the stage direction "Lights out" between "known" and "Sharers of"). MS does not copy quotation but reads "*Read p. 74 *Sometime sharers of the same house . . . in silence understood* *."
7. *EA* 11–12. MS does not copy quotation but reads "**Read *There is the city*, p. 75**."
8. *EA*, 12. MS does not copy quotation but reads "**Read p. 76, *to throw away the key***"; Jarrell may have gone on to read the rest of the chorus's speech (some twenty more lines).
9. MS reads here: "**Read *On Cautly* (??), p. 79, and after first two lines on top of page 80 interrupt to say:"
10. So *Poems* (1934), 79–80; *EA*, 14 differs slightly.
11. MS has a closed parenthesis here, but no open parenthesis before "The easy way." MS continues: "Now go on, read through *Enough to have lightly touched the unworthy thing*."
12. *EA*, 14–15.
13. *EA*, 15. MS does not quote but reads "Read * p. 82 *The Spring will come . . .* *."
14. *EA*, 17. MS reads "**Read p. 85, *Now we have seen***."
15. *EA*, 17. MS reads "**Read p. 85**."
16. Note that this sentence (1) confirms that Jarrell used, or at least planned, the *Paid on Both Sides* material for the lectures, and also (2) helps place the material within the sequence of the lectures, which

it in turn helps to construct: Jarrell must have talked about *Paid on Both Sides* after a lecture that covered psychoanalytic material (but this could be lecture 1, lecture 3, or lecture 5).

17. Polar bear: "The Tale of Audun from the West Fjords," trans. Anthony Maxwell, in *The Complete Sagas of Icelanders*, vol. 1, ed. Vidar Hreinsson et al. (Reykjavik: Leifur Eiriksson, 1997), 369–74. *The Cocktail Party*: T. S. Eliot's 1950 verse play. *The Witch Is Not for Burning*: Jarrell's error for *The Lady's Not for Burning*; see note 19 on Christopher Fry, below.

18. "What I worked out is substantially what I have continued to employ: a line of varying length and varying number of syllables, with a caesura and three stresses. The caesura and the stresses may come at different places, almost anywhere in the line; the stresses may be close together or well separate by light syllables; the only rule being that there must be one stress on one side of the caesura and two on the other." T. S. Eliot, "Poetry and Drama" (1951), in *On Poetry and Poets* (New York: Farrar, Straus and Cudahy, 1957), 88.

19. The English playwright Christopher Fry (born 1907) enjoyed transatlantic success after the Second World War with verse plays such as *The Lady's Not for Burning* (1948) and *Venus Observed* (1949).

20. "The rhythm of regular blank verse had become too remote from the movement of modern speech. . . . An avoidance of too much iambic, some use of alliteration, and occasional unexpected rhyme helped to distinguish the versification [in *Murder in the Cathedral*] from that of the nineteenth century." Eliot, "Poetry and Drama," 85.

21. William Shakespeare, *Macbeth* 5:5:17–28; *Troilus and Cressida* 3:3:145–190; probably *Measure for Measure* 3:1:5–41 (line numbers from *The Riverside Shakespeare*, ed. G. Blakemore Evans et al. [Boston: Houghton Mifflin, 1974]).

22. *CP*, xxv (reprinted from *Collected Poetry* 1945).

23. Perse: Saint-John Perse (Aléxis Saint-Léger Léger, 1887–1975) whose "Asiatic" lists make an important feature of his prose poem *Anabase* (1942); both Auden and Eliot translated his work.

24. *EA*, 70–71. Jarrell has crossed out the following sentence, which reads: "Whenever I read Gertrude Stein my limbs grow heavy, my eyeballs start to roll back in my head, and I think foolishly: why, *I* could write this well; since all that happens to me whenever I read this passage, I think that it has been influenced by Gertrude Stein."

25. Jarrell has cancelled "hearers of these lectures" and replaced it, in pen, with "you my readers"; he has also written, in pencil, "rev. for book," clearly revisions made after the lectures were given.

26. *EA*, 93; Jarrell omits Auden's line for paragraph breaks.

27. *EA*, 94. In *The Orators* (1932) E. is apparently male (see *EA*, 86); the version of *The Orators* in *Collected Poetry* 1945 makes E. a girl instead.

28. *EA*, 106, 98, 109.

29. Jarrell's discussion of *New Year Letter* draws on his initial review of the poem and the volume which contained it, *The Double Man*, published in *The Nation*, April 12, 1941, and reprinted in *Kipling, Auden, and Co.* (New York: Farrar, Straus and Giroux, 1980), 55–57.

30. Samuel Butler composed his satirical, anti-Puritan narrative poem *Hudibras* (1663–1678) in the rapid, jaunty couplets now called (after the poem) hudibrastics. *Critique of Judgment*: the 1790 work of philosophy by Immanuel Kant.

31. Jarrell appears to be paraphrasing, rather than quoting, a central idea for Kierkegaard's writings on ethics: compare, for example, "an aesthetic choice is no choice. The act of choosing is essentially a proper and stringent expression of the ethical." Søren Kierkegaard, *Either/Or*, vol. 2, trans. Walter Lowrie (Princeton, N.J.: Princeton University Press, 1946), 141.

32. *CP*, 292; Jarrell has added his own quotation marks.

33. *Collected Poetry* 1945, 261–62; *CP*, 294 strips the title and changes punctuation slightly. I print the 1945 version. MS reads "a typical one, The Adventurers: read on page 261."

34. The MS page beginning with this sentence and coextensive with its paragraph (ending "interesting ideas") is written on Princeton University stationery, as the rest of the lectures are not; it is also the last in the 7a . . . 7d sequence. The MS as the Berg Collection preserves it continues with "Auden calls 'The Sea and the Mirror' "," the page numbered 8. In a chronological discussion of Auden's long poems, "For the Time Being" would belong between *The Quest* and the postwar poems (*The Age of Anxiety*, "The Sea and the Mirror"); I have therefore placed the discussion of "For the Time Being" after the end of this paragraph.

35. This paragraph about "For the Time Being" survives as an independent, one-page MS in the ninth of the nine folders at the Berg Collection.

36. *Macbeth* 5:1:40.
37. *CP*, 405; properly "all that we are not stares back at what we are."
38. *CP*, 407.
39. Jarrell has cancelled the end of this sentence, from "Antonio stands for" to "are concerned," and marked it "CHANGE"; since the MS offers no alternative, I take the cancellation as post-1952.
40. *CP*, 409 (properly, "all around my life").
41. *CP*, 409.
42. See lecture 5, note 16.
43. *CP*, 409 (properly, "Is but a robbers' ambush); set as prose in MS, with virgules separating lines ("good music / In shocking taste," etc.).
44. *CP*, 412, 411 (properly, "mentor, / The grown-up").
45. *CP*, 412; square brackets in the preceding line as in MS; quote marks around the single quoted line in MS. Here and below Jarrell sometimes sets off a one- or two-line quote as he would a longer quotation; one- and two-line quotations are here integrated into paragraph text.
46. *CP*, 415; quote marks around the quoted couplet in MS.
47. *CP*, 420; quote marks around the last two quoted lines in MS.
48. *CP* 420–21.
49. The MS the Berg Collection preserves as lecture 6 breaks off here.
50. *CP*, 444. The paragraph imitates Auden's "Caliban" style; it quotes Auden only as indicated by single quotes (at the end of the paragraph). MS opens the paragraph with ordinary double quotes (") but neglects to close them; closing double quote mark here is an editorial emendation.
51. The sentence in MS ends "description of The World of Childhood p. 393' " (with a double quote mark after "393"). This paragraph, and the paragraph before it (beginning "'Real life . . . ") represent one MS page in folder 9; on the reverse of the page, Jarrell has written, in very large letters, "CALIBAN." Page 393 of *Collected Poetry* 1945, part of "Caliban to the Audience," runs from "stop will be far outside" to "sunset glittered on," corresponding to most of *CP*, 437; Jarrell evidently read aloud part or all of the second half of this page (beginning " 'Release us,' you will beg," and preceded by a row of asterisks) which indeed describes "The World of Childhood"; the excerpt printed here represents a best guess.
52. These last paragraphs of lecture 6 as I reconstruct it (from "Audience, your questions" to "intolerable") the Berg Collection has filed

apart from Jarrell's material on Auden, as "comments on Shakespeare's *The Tempest*"; they plainly conclude a discussion of "The Sea and the Mirror."

53. This sentence (beginning "Life is") appears in the MS margin.

54. *CP*, 439.

55. The pre-Socratic philosopher Parmenides of Elea argued that change and time were illusions, and the real world, a static singularity.

56. Again, Jarrell imitates Auden's "Caliban" style. MS here has a close quote (") after "intolerable," but no corresponding open quote, nor does the concluding series of adjectival phrases represent a quotation from Auden; Jarrell appears to have underlined them for emphasis.

Index

Titles for Auden's book-length works appear in the index as separate entries; titles for Auden's shorter poems appear only when the lectures discuss them at length.

"Spain 1937" (Auden), 13, 66–70, 76,
130, 153, 155n2, 162n21
Spears, Monroe, 5, 140n43
Spencer, Herbert, 20, 143n3
Spender, Stephen, 13, 45, 150n40
Spinoza, Baruch (Benedict), 87
Stalin, Josef, 34, 68, 91, 97, 147n2
Stauffer, Donald, 8, 139n27
Stead, Christina, 145n24
Stein, Gertrude, 124, 166n24
Stendhal (Henri Beyle), 72, 76,
156n14
Sullivan, Sir Arthur. See Gilbert,
W. S., and Arthur Sullivan
Swift, Jonathan, 40, 126, 148n22
Swinburne, Algernon Charles, 21,
143n5

Tarski, Alfred, 98, 162n23
Tate, Allen, xiii, 1, 4
Taylor, Peter, 151n11
Tchaikovsky, Pyotr Ilyich, 57, 67
technique (verse technique). See
Auden, W. H., verse technique; see
also professions and professionalism
Tempest, The (Shakespeare). See
Shakespeare, William; see also "Sea
and the Mirror, The" (Auden)
Tennyson, Alfred, Lord, 72; "Locks-
ley Hall," 57, 143n5, 152n25
Thomas, Dylan, 157n20
Thomas, Edward, 36
Thomson, Virgil, 66, 154–55n1
"Through the Looking Glass"
(Auden), 28
"To a Nightingale" (Keats), 79
"To a Wild-Fowl" (William Cullen
Bryant), 19

Tolkien, J. R. R., 21
Tolstoy, Leo, 130
"Too Dear, Too Vague" (Auden), 26
Trotsky, Leon, 24, 145n16

uncles, 29, 39–40, 45–46, 91, 124–25
"Under Sirius" (Auden), 82, 158n39
"Under Which Lyre" (Auden), xiii,
141n45
Untermeyer, Louis, 89, 125, 160n8
Upward, Edward, 125

Vanderbilt University, 1, 3
"Vanity of Human Wishes, The"
(Johnson), x
"Venus Will Now Say a Few Words"
(Auden), 26
Victory at Sea (Rodgers), ix
votes and voting, 86, 88, 95, 103

Warren, Robert Penn, xiii, 1, 3
Wells, H. G., 35
"When you and I were all" (Jarrell), 2
Whitman, Walt, 10, 56
Williams, William Carlos, 10,
138n22
wit, xi–xiv, 71, 126–28
Wordsworth, William, 56, 72,
156n12
Woman's College of North Carolina
(Greensboro), 6
Wozzeck (Buchner), 119

Yale Review, 13, 141n46, 154
Yeats, William Butler, xiii, 3, 21, 55,
72, 121, 131, 143n6, 160n3

Zabel, Morton Dauwen, 5

Further Acknowledgments

Excerpts from "A Dialogue between Soul and Body," "The Difficult Resolu-
tion," and "When you and I were all" from *The Complete Poems* by Randall Jarrell.
Copyright © 1969, renewed 1997 by Mary von S. Jarrell. Reprinted by per-
mission of Farrar, Straus and Giroux, LLC.

Excerpts from poems by W. H. Auden and Randall Jarrell reprinted by per-
mission of Faber and Faber Ltd.

"Orpheus. Euridice. Hermes" from *Selected Works* Vol. II by Rainer Maria Rilke
and translated by J. B. Leishman and published by The Hogarth Press. Used by
permission of St. John's College, Oxford and The Random House Group Lim-
ited. (UK)

"Too Dear, Too Vague," copyright © 1976 by Edward Mendelson, William
Meredith and Monroe K. Spears, Executors of the Estate of W. H. Auden.,
"Heavy Date," copyright 1945 by W. H. Auden, "The Prophets," copyright ©
1976 by Edward Mendelson, William Meredith and Monroe K. Spears, Execu-
tors of the Estate of W. H. Auden., "Meiosis", copyright © 1976 by Edward
Mendelson, William Meredith and Monroe K. Spears, Executors of the Estate
of W. H. Auden., "September 1, 1939" copyright 1940 & renewed 1968 by
W. H. Auden, "As He Is", copyright 1940 & renewed 1968 by W. H. Auden,
"Dover", copyright © 1976 by Edward Mendelson, William Meredith and
Monroe K. Spears, Executors of the Estate of W. H. Auden., "A Misunder-
standing", copyright © 1976 by Edward Mendelson, William Meredith and
Monroe K. Spears, Executors of the Estate of W. H. Auden., "New Year Letter",
copyright 1941 & renewed 1969 by W. H. Auden, "Rimbaud", copyright 1940
& renewed 1968 by W. H. Auden, "The Novelist", copyright 1940 and renewed
1968 by W. H. Auden, "In Memory of W. B. Yeats", copyright 1940 & renewed
1968 by W. H. Auden, "In Memory of Sigmund Freud", copyright 1940 and re-
newed 1968 by W. H. Auden, "In Sickness and In Health", copyright 1945 by
W. H. Auden, "The Age of Anxiety", copyright 1947 by W. H. Auden & re-
newed 1975 by the Estate of W. H. Auden, "For the Time Being", copyright
1944 and renewed 1972 by W. H. Auden, "Horae Canonicae", copyright ©
1976 by Edward Mendelson, William Meredith and Monroe K. Spears, Execu-
tors of the Estate of W. H. Auden., "Their Lonely Betters", copyright 1951 by
W. H. Auden, "The Chimaeras", copyright © 1976 by Edward Mendelson,
William Meredith and Monroe K. Spears, Executors of the Estate of W. H. Au-
den., "A Household", copyright 1951 by W. H. Auden, "Letter to Lord Byron",
copyright 1937 by W. H. Auden, "Paid on Both Sides", copyright 1934 by The
Modern Library, Inc., & renewed 1962 by W. H. Auden, "The Quest", copyright
© 1976 by Edward Mendelson, William Meredith and Monroe K. Spears, Ex-
ecutors of the Estate of W. H. Auden., "The Sea and the Mirror", copyright ©
1976 by Edward Mendelson, William Meredith and Monroe K. Spears, Execu-
tors of the Estate of W. H. Auden., from *Collected Poems* by W. H. Auden. Used
by permission of Random House, Inc.